The Complete Guide to Successful Trading Business

By

Paul M King

First edition published in 2007.

ISBN: 978-0-6151-3768-1

Published by:

PMKing Trading LLC, Middlebury, VT, 05753
www.pmkingtrading.com
Edition 1.9 1/29/7

For Wendy and Josh - the inspiration for everything I do.

The Complete Guide to Building a Successful Trading Business

by

Paul M King

Table of Contents

Table of Figures

Narrative Entries

Acknowledgements

This book would not have been possible without the help of the following people:

Many thanks go to my wife Wendy for looking after our son Josh and allowing me the time to write this book. (You also did a great job of the proofreading by the way). Thanks for tirelessly and meticulously putting up with reading all my endless trading-related publications, electronic books, and articles and for the time I spent writing rather than being with you and Josh.

Thanks to all my trading mentor clients all over the world – without your questions, comments, praise, and passion for trading I would not be able to find the inspiration and dedication to write a book like this. I hope you find this book as useful to your trading as I have found writing it to mine.

Many thanks go to everybody at the Van Tharp Institute. Your truly excellent publications, products, and services have been helping traders, including myself and my clients, be the very best they can possibly be for more than 25 years.

All the participants on Van Tharp's MasterMind™ Trading forum – your questions, comments, (and occasional disagreement and ranting) give me endless inspiration and reward for the work I do in the trading business and I never tire of spending my time attempting to help people with their trading-related problems online on the forum.

What are you doing with your life?

September 11th 2001, Manhattan, New York

It is a beautiful fall day; bright blue sky, yellowing leaves. It was the kind of day that made it a pleasure to get the ferry to work from Fair Haven, New Jersey to Manhattan. I was on the "lazy boat" that got me to work in the Reuters Building in Times Square way later than usual but I didn't really care – everything at the office would keep until I got there.

I'd decided to read the New York Times inside the boat instead of sitting on the top deck to get some fresh air. We were going under the Verrazano-Narrows Bridge when the first plane hit the World Trade Center and everything changed.

The TVs on the boat were tuned to CNN and it said a plane had hit. Everyone assumed a small single seat plane had gone off-course until we looked out of the window and saw the flames, the massive gaping hole visible even from that distance, and the huge black plume of smoke.

We docked, and the boat got crammed full of scared and bewildered people and it headed straight back to New Jersey. Nobody even considered getting off when we docked. The skyline of Manhattan had been changed forever by the time we got back to the Jersey shore and I was met by Wendy, my wife. Everyone filed off the boat in stunned silence and went home to watch the news for 5 days straight.

People I knew were killed. Everyone knew someone who was missing. I thought "What am I doing with my life?" and "Would I have left any kind of lasting memory if I had died?"

The seeds of PMKing Trading were sown in my head. I was determined to "do something", I just didn't know what right then. Working in Manhattan was never the same after that day for me.

♛ Introduction

Many people would say 'If you are already a successful trader with a profitable trading company, why would you write a book to tell other people how to do what you have done?' The simple answer is that when I decided to create a successful trading business there was no single book that offered a complete solution to what I needed to do; so I decided to write one. I did not know if I would publish it when it was finished – I just knew that if I wrote it, then my own trading would be significantly improved and I would know I had 'covered all the bases'. I also knew that I would eventually want to employ people to help grow my trading business and I would need an 'employee manual' to help me explain the philosophy behind my business.

The more complex answer is that in doing the work to write this book, my trading and coaching has improved dramatically because I have been encouraged to think very deeply about every single aspect of my trading business and why I created it the way I did. This is similar to the revelations I get when I answer other trader's questions on online trading forums or coach people to be better traders. I have been contributing to one particular forum for a few years now (and recently became an official host there) and I am sure it has improved my trading much more than the other participant's trading has been improved by my answers. An internet search for "MasterMind Forum" should get you there.

In writing this book I learned one major thing about building a successful trading business, and that is if you really, truly love trading, and have an open mind about learning how to do it well, then you can succeed – given the right information and preparation. I also realized that the things that make a trading business successful are all 'learnable' – there is no secret magic involved - and that the markets are big enough for us all to succeed. I live by the old Chinese philosophy that 'people who say a thing is impossible should not interrupt those doing it'. You can succeed if you know what is important and what is not. That's what this book is about.

Lastly, in case you are hoping for the magic formula or trading system to be revealed here, you will be very disappointed. Success is not about a trade entry signal, and if you think that is the important aspect of building a successful trading business then just stop reading now and subscribe to one of the many 'win on every trade' newsletters that fill up your email inbox every day. Building any successful business is about hard work, good planning, and more hard work. This book is intended to tell you what exactly it is you should be working hard on to be a success - in as complete and detailed way as possible.

In attempting to cover a complex subject, such as building a trading business, it is inevitable that I cannot go into as much detail as I would have liked in every single aspect. In these cases I have concentrated on completeness rather than detail and have hopefully given enough context and background information to allow the reader to research the area in more detail using other recommended sources where applicable.

For more information or to ask specific questions about this book, or trading in general, please use the contact page on my web site at:

www.pmkingtrading.com

Wishing you success in your trading.

Paul King, , 22nd August 2006, Middlebury, Vermont.

What This Book Will Teach You

This book is split in to 3 main sections that deal with the main areas of building a trading business:

Part I   - The Opening: Business Management
Part II   - The Middle Game: Trading System Management
Part III - The End Game: Trader Management

Each section is relatively independent and could be read in any order. A section on managing other people's money has not been included – maybe that will come in a later book when I am more experienced in that particular aspect of trading. Since **Trading System Management** is obviously much more exciting than the other sections there is always a tendency to place more emphasis on this section and neglect the others. This would be a big mistake. Although creating a successful, profitable, robust suite of trading systems is essential to the success of the business - since this is the thing that creates the income - unless you have good business management and planning, and understand your trading psychology so you make few implementation errors, you will not be successful overall.

Once you have read this book you will understand, and be aware of, everything that you need to consider in order to build a successful trading business. Although this book intends to cover everything you need, laws and regulations change regularly. In some cases the book will recommend that you get professional advice before making certain decisions, and in those cases the book should just be used as a guide to your possible choices, and to give you a reasonable level of understanding before consulting with a professional. This book cannot, and should not be used instead of consulting a professional who specializes in the subject matter, and will be up to date on all legal and regulatory considerations for your particular situation.

♔ What This Book Won't Teach You

This book will not teach you a foolproof way to make money, any specific trading systems that PMKing Trading currently uses, and will not instantly transform you into a profitable trader if you are currently a losing one.

Almost every other book about trading that exists concentrates on the actual trading systems that the author uses (or used to use), or just some (supposedly) highly profitable entry signals in specific markets. The business of trading, and the reasons why a good system in the hands of an ill-prepared trader will lose money are usually completely neglected. This book does not attempt to tell you which system to use; instead it tells you how to develop trading systems that suit you personally, and how they should be implemented in the context of a good business plan.

Other things this book does not tell you (just so you are not disappointed at the end):

- How to set up a legal entity in your specific jurisdiction or country
- How to do your business accounting and tax reporting
- How your broker's order entry software or interface works
- How to automate your trading system in any specific programming language or trading system development platform
- How to win on every trade
- How to get rich, quickly, with little effort
- How to make money without taking any calculated risks

If you need to know the answers to anything on the above list, It is suggested that you buy one of the many other books about trading and put this one back on the shelf. If you've already purchased this book, then oh well, why not read it anyway? You might just learn something you didn't know. If you already understand that the answers to the questions above are not the key things that will allow you to build a successful trading business then 'Congratulations!' you are already ahead of the game compared to most of the other people in this business. Read on, and discover what you really need to know and do to be successful.

Planning? What planning?

Spring 2002, Manhattan, New York

Life goes on. I still have a good job; a business analyst in the Analytical Trading department of a leading Electronic Communication Network (ECN) in Manhattan. It's a two hour commute on the ferry from Fair Haven, New Jersey, but the pay is pretty good, the work is challenging and the ferry has a bar for the trip home. The company is also sponsoring me for permanent residence in the United States so I can remain here with my family and continue the life we've built.

Suddenly everything changed. The company gets into a huge price war with a major (newer, smaller, but much leaner) competitor. Trading commission revenue is slashed from highs that it will never see again and the whole trading environment is turned on its head. Okay, not so bad, I'm in a department that is relatively unaffected, and it's the old legacy charge-10c-per-share business that's gone down the toilet. We can evolve, we can stay calm, we can get through this.

It rapidly gets worse. People start getting fired left and right. Still, I'm untouched, our department is well respected. Nobody wants me to leave. Unfortunately the US Immigration and Nationalization Service has other ideas. People have been fired, American people, US Citizens damn it. If any of them can theoretically do my job then I can't get permanent residence. Once my visa has expired I'm on the next flight home to the UK.

What should I do? Go back home? No, I don't want to do that. I like working in Manhattan, I have a new son (he's got no problems, he was born here so he doesn't have visa issues, but he's only 3 months old so it's 20 years and 9 months until he can sponsor us to stay in the US). I've made a life out here now for over 5 years. I want to make it work. I know, I'll quit my job and start a business and get a visa that way. It shouldn't be too hard. What kind of business? Why not trading? I know a thing or two about that business. Everything else I've ever done has been a relative 'piece of cake' so far. Making money buying and selling stuff shouldn't be too much of a stretch. Does anyone know a trustworthy immigration attorney?

PMKing Trading is born July 1st 2002

Part I – The Opening: Business Management

If you don't have a business plan you don't really have a business; it's as simple as that.

The successful operation of any business, not just a trading business, is about two key things:

1. Positive cash flow
2. Positive balance sheet

A successful business has income that is greater than the expense of running the business, and a balance sheet where assets are greater than liabilities. Income should gradually increase, expenses should increase slower than income, assets should increase, and liabilities should decrease over time. The important areas of business management include:

- Planning
- Setup costs
- Cash Flow
- Client Management
- Vendor Management
- Employee Management
- Technology Management
- Accounting, Legal and Regulatory Issues

For a trading business some of these areas are more complex than a regular business (due to the unpredictable nature of the cash flow), and some are much simpler (due to having an intangible product and digital inventory). Each of these areas will now be covered in detail. Some of the material is generic and can be applied to any business startup, but most of it is specific to starting and operating a trading business.

Although it is much easier to start a trading business than most other enterprises - you already have a brokerage account now right? You could start trading immediately if you're not already? Finishing one is the difficult thing. Operation costs can be low, digital inventory is easy to manage, but the unpredictability of weekly, monthly, and even yearly income streams make things difficult to plan and operate effectively even for an established business.

Your business management and planning has to be much more detailed and superior to other business ventures to ensure you can "weather the storm" financially and psychologically. You need to be able to survive through the turbulent times in order to reap the benefits of the good times.

Having said all that, trading is one of the few businesses where startup costs are low, and how much you make is generally proportional to the size of your trading account, not how hard you work. Once you have done all the hard work to create your suite of trading systems, the amount of income you generate is simply proportional to the size you trade and the risk you take. The business is virtually unlimited in scalability if you design your trading methods correctly. There are few other businesses where the same amount of hard work can generate virtually unlimited income with only a small amount of incremental effort.

The following sections are the most important ones in this book; they are also the most tedious to work though, and difficult to get motivated to actually complete – who wants to write a business plan when they could be making money trading? As with many things in life, the tasks that are most difficult, boring, tedious, or simply uninteresting are the ones that are critical to success and will be the thing that distinguishes the winners from the losers. Good planning is not hard; it is just not interesting like trading system development, or actual trading. If you don't have a plan, you don't have a business – you just have a random collection of events within the structure of a legal entity. Your chances of long-term success are virtually zero. Remember you are always competing with the rest of the trading community for those elusive trading profits, and if you have no plan and someone else does who do you think is going to win more often by being consistent?

Think about competing in an online chess tournament against the best Grandmasters and chess computers in the world. How well do you think you would do if you 'just started playing'? Compare that approach to someone who has researched chess strategy, memorized key openings, rehearsed key concepts of the game, understands the different phases of the game, and has practiced tirelessly, all in the context of a specific plan for success.

🐎 Business Planning

A business plan is the very first thing you need to do, and the great news is that it doesn't cost anything except your time and effort. If the thought of doing this is boring, or you think you can 'fill in the gaps' after you have started trading, this would be a big mistake. If you are already trading, and don't have a business plan then my advice would be this:

STOP TRADING, INVESTING, OR RISKING YOUR CAPITAL RIGHT NOW!

The single most significant reason why your trading business could fail is because you have a cash flow problem and cannot continue to operate the business and pay all your business and personal expenses. It doesn't matter how many profitable trading systems you have if you can't continue to trade them. This problem can be avoided by doing a complete business plan. This helps to ensure that you do not start a business where you have to raid your trading account after six months to pay the mortgage - or cease operation simply because you lose money trading for six months in a row or even a year. These kind of losing periods are perfectly normal – especially in the first years of trading where you are the worst trader you'll ever be.

Imagine you have to pitch this business idea to a venture capitalist (or at least your spouse) and you need a convincing, detailed, sensible, realistic plan to present. Your plan should answer the following questions:

Feasibility Goals and Objectives

Why are you starting a trading business?
Why should you succeed where others have failed?
What is your edge?
What are you trying to achieve?
What percentage return per year is reasonable?
What percentage loss is acceptable?
What constitutes success and failure?
How long are you allowing before trading becomes consistently profitable?

Setup

How will you fund the setup costs?
Where is your initial risk capital coming from?
What resources will you use for legal advice, accounting advice, and tax planning advice?
What criteria will you use to evaluate a broker?
What hardware, software, and other office setup items will you need?
Where will you trade?
How are you going to find the time to build and operate the business?

Cash Flow

How will you cover personal and business expenses while the trading business is being developed?
Do you need to make money immediately?
Where is your emergency reserve?
Where is the operational money coming from?
What will your monthly operational expenses be?
How will you continue operations through sustained draw-downs (in size and time)?

Trading Systems

What kind of systems do you need?
What timeframe will suit your personality?
What technology or programming skills will you need to implement your systems?
What markets will you trade?
What is your backup for every component of your trading environment in case of failure?
When is a trading system broken and should be suspended?
What types of market does your system work in?
What instrument are you going to trade?
Are your systems highly correlated or diversified?

Operations and Management

Will you continue to do your regular job or be dedicated to the trading business full-time?
Who will manage your business?
Who will do the accounting?
Who will track expense?
Who will track trades?
What are your emergency plans if you are unable to trade?
What circumstances would cause you to cease operations and re-evaluate the business?
What professional advisors do you need?
How will you manage failure?
How will you manage success?

Once you have read and completed the following sections, and written your business plan, you should check off the list above to make sure you have a satisfactory and detailed answer to each of the questions before proceeding to **Part II** of this book which covers the subject of **Trading System Management**.

If you haven't, can't, or won't complete a trading business plan, then this would be a big red flag to proceeding with this whole business. There is something wrong with your motivation, your circumstances, or your personality that is preventing you from completing this essential step to success. I would strongly advise you to find out what is holding you back before you invest any more time, effort, or money into trading. You are setting yourself up to fail in a classic example of 'self sabotage'.

Some reasons that you might be struggling with creating your plan:

- Impatience to get to the 'making money' part
- Fear of discovering that building a trading business is not right or even possible for you
- Plain old laziness
- You have other more important things to do

This book does come with one guarantee, and it is this:

If you do not get to the root cause of your hesitation to finish a trading business plan, your business will never succeed no matter what you do to develop, test, and implement any trading systems.

At some point your confidence and dedication to the business will be severely tested, and without the backup that a complete business plan gives you, you won't pass the test. Either you'll give up after a losing period, decide it isn't really possible to have a successful trading business, or blame it all on someone or something else and quit a loser.

Most people are much more suited to the regular safety of a pre-defined, periodic paycheck, rather than the calculated risk and responsibility of owning their own business; maybe you are one of those people. If you cannot create a business plan, then you are really telling yourself that 'trading is not for me'. That is fine – at least you have not lost a lot of money to find this out! Look for something else that you love and build a business around that. Passion is the driving force for anything that is not simple to achieve and if you don't have it, you won't be able to create a plan. You should find something else that does excite and motivate you.

How not to do it

Fall 2002, Fair Haven, New Jersey

I am now the proud owner of my own 3-month-old trading business: PMKing Trading LLC. Ten grand (the answer's always at least ten grand, inflation adjusted of course, no matter what the question is) to an immigration attorney and I can get a visa to stay in the US through my company. An attorney to do the legal work, an accountant to do the tax returns, a trading account with $50,000 in it and I'm all set to go.

Let's see now, how do our finances look? We live in an expensive house in an expensive neighborhood, with expensive bills and huge property taxes. We're not extravagant (we only have one car even though we have a double garage) but our monthly expenses are about $6000. That means we need about $75,000 in after-tax income to stay afloat, which means about $150,000 in gross income (just to be on the safe side) so I only need to make 300% per year from my trading to make it all add up.

That shouldn't be a problem for an intelligent, motivated, business analyst with a home office, a computer, and a wife and seven month old baby son in the house. Now, what should I trade? Options maybe, I know they can make you lots of cash. I'll need to trade inexpensive ones so I can buy enough to really make a good profit. How about some puts? My extensive analysis, conducted over the last three months, tells me that the markets are all definitely heading down the toilet. All I need to do is buy a load of out-of-the-money puts and watch the cash roll in.

I'm up $1000 in a day. Not bad. If I can just do that for each of the 250 trading days a year everything will be just fine. I'm a little concerned about the risk I'm taking[1], but I know what I'm doing, I'll just get out if things don't go too well.

The markets start to go up gradually and volatility decreases significantly; the absolute kiss of death to long put positions. In no time I'm down $20,000, 40% of my starting capital has vanished. I feel sick, I'm sweating, my eyes are blurry, I can't think, but I'm still in my positions. I get scared. Not of the money I lost, but of the thought that if this is what it feels like to lose money trading then I can't be in this business. It'll kill me. I can't be in a business that makes me feel like this every time I have a losing position.

---

[1] In fact I was trading at a size that I wouldn't trade now even if I had an account 10 times what it was then

It turns out I have a stomach bug and the symptoms were from the illness not the trading. My wife is horrified at the $20,000 loss and says "Why don't you just get out, especially if you're sick?" I think that's what she said; the actual words are a little hazy. I get out of my positions. The loss is realized.

I'm down 40% in the first 3 months of trading. How did that happen? Quickly, that's how. Lucky I had the wife-stop or I'd probably have lost a lot more.

So much for Mister-Genius-Piece-of-Cake-Business-Analyst-Hot-Shot-Trader. Maybe I should read a book that tells me how to build a successful trading business before carrying on? Anyone know any good trading business development books?

♞ Feasibility and Objectives

Many people think that this section of your business plan is obvious – 'I want to be rich'. That is much too simplistic to be useful (and what exactly is 'rich' anyway?) It is worth spending a lot of time on this section of your plan to make sure you really know why you are setting yourself up for all this work, and exactly what you are trying to achieve.

Firstly, how much time can you dedicate to doing all of this? If you have a full-time job and a family, where is the 'spare' time to plan and build a business coming from? Can you afford to quit your full-time job and rely on some other income to pay personal expenses while you start to grow a business? It is good to err on the side of caution, and I would make an assumption that the trading business will not be cash-flow positive for a number of years. How will you ensure your personal financial survival during this period?

Sometimes you can have fortunate circumstances that conspire to make you come to the decision that starting a trading business is the only sensible thing for you to do. For example, if you quit a well-paying, full-time job and got a severance package, sold a house that had significantly appreciated in value, and moved to Vermont to reduce monthly personal expenses it would probably be a fortunate turn of events indeed[2]. This would give you a lower monthly expense basis, a stack of cash to see you through the initial losing months, and a very good incentive to make the business work!

Most people are not fortunate enough to have these kinds of opportunities handed to them on a plate, and that is what makes the planning stage of your business so much more important. Planning and desire are the only things that can create an environment in which your business can be born and flourish.

In the case of PMKing Trading, I was willing to completely change my life to give the trading business the best chance of success, and I also had a spouse that was willing to take the risks along with me. Do you have the same opportunity and support to give your business the best chance of success?

---

[2] This is almost exactly (but not quite) how PMKing Trading was started

Next come objectives. What exactly are you trying to achieve? For PMKing Trading, the initial objectives were as follows:

- Maintain legal residency in US
- Provide a decent standard of living for the owners
- Give clients an alternative investment vehicle
- Provide financial advice to improve people's standard of living
- Positively impact the local economy
- Create employment for local people
- Give family a good return on their investments

Each of these objectives needs to be quantified so they can be measured, and this is what differentiates a simple 'to-do' list from real goals. For example, 'a decent standard of living' needs to be defined by quantifying it and putting a timeframe on it to turn it into a measurable goal.

For example:

A decent standard of living is defined as passive net income (i.e. income not directly worked for, after taxes and other business expenses) from the trading business is sufficient to cover twice the normal monthly living expenses of the owner(s).

It is very important that you are realistic in your goal setting – having a goal that says you will make 100% return per year with no more than a 10% drawdown is not sensible, and you will only be disappointed. Risk and reward always go together. On the flip side, make sure your goals are a real challenge since it is amazing to me how often one attains what one sets out to do. Set the bar high (but not impossibly high) so that achieving your goals has a real and significant positive impact on your life. It may actually be an interesting revelation to you what your goals actually turn out to be when you think about them – it might even be the case that you can achieve them without actually starting a trading business. If this is true I would heartily recommend that you don't put yourself through the time and effort required to build a successful trading business and 'take the easy way out'. Why achieve your objectives the hard way?

♟ Business Setup

Once you know what you are trying to achieve, it is much easier to define how your business should be set up. It is possible to 'just start trading' in a personal brokerage account, but investigating and choosing a legal entity structure for your trading is definitely worthwhile. Even if you ultimately decide that you do not want to set up a business, it is very useful to know why you made that choice, and what you are giving up by not having a separate legal entity for your trading. Note that in all cases United States law and terminology is used. Please check with a licensed professional regarding your particular circumstances before creating a legal entity in your country or jurisdiction.

There are 5 main choices for your legal entity structure within which you will perform your trading activity and manage your trading business. The choices are:

1. Individual
2. Sole Proprietor
3. Partnership
4. Corporation (C or S)
5. Limited Liability Company (LLC)

The main criteria used when selecting a legal entity include:

- Ease of setup and management
- Liability Protection
- Tax Considerations
- Income Flexibility

Each of the choices will be considered in terms of the main criteria, and then a recommendation will be made depending on which of the criteria is most important to you.

♟ Individual

The simplest choice you can make is to effectively "do nothing" and simply trade in an individual brokerage account. Ease of setup and management is the only advantage to doing this (since you are already setup to trade as an individual if you already have a brokerage account). If you want to trade other people's money, have any kind of liability protection for your personal assets separate from your trading assets, have any favorable tax treatment for your trading expenses, or any income flexibility when it comes to trading profits, then trading as an individual is not a good choice.

⚹ Sole Proprietor

Electing to trade as a Sole Proprietor is basically an accounting decision. No separate legal entity is created (even though you can trade under a name that is separate from your own name) so the setup and management of this choice is minimal. The main advantage is that you are able to deduct certain trading-related expenses from any profits you make before taxes are calculated. Being a sole proprietor does not give you any kind of liability protection, and you do not have any flexibility when it comes to the treatment of your trading profits – they are automatically included on your personal tax return as income. Since a sole proprietor is not a separate legal entity from the owner, the owner's death would automatically terminate the sole proprietorship.

⚹ Partnership

There are 3 types of partnership:

- General Partnership (GP)
- Limited Partnership (LP)
- Limited Liability Partnership (LLP)

The main advantage of a partnership is that it allows more than one person to own and make decisions for the business.

A **General Partnership** is not a separate legal entity and does not protect the partners from the firm's debts or obligations. It is dissolved on the death of a partner.

A **Limited Partnership** is a separate legal entity, but the general partner(s) still have unlimited liability. This is generally a good choice for an entity within which to manage other people's money (like a hedge fund) with the trader(s) as the general partner(s), and the clients as the limited partners. This book is primarily concerned with the legal entity selection for your *main* trading entity so applicability to hedge fund setup is not a consideration.

A **Limited Liability Partnership** does offer liability protection for all general partners but will be dissolved if a partner leaves (not just dies).

Corporation

A corporation is a separate legal entity that has an Employer Identification Number (EIN) which is the corporate equivalent of your social security number. A corporation must be created at the federal and state level with the appropriate paperwork and is subject to formal procedures and regulations. These include having a board of directors, annual meetings, minutes for corporate resolutions and decisions, and special accounting and tax reporting rules. Therefore the setup and maintenance of a corporation is a more significant undertaking.

Since the corporation is a separate legal entity, your personal assets are protected from corporate liability assuming you maintain the legal status of the corporation. There are 2 main kinds of corporation:

- C Corporation
- S Corporation

Each will now be described.

C Corporation

The C Corporation is the most common kind of corporation structure. The main disadvantage of a C Corporation (apart from the formal regulatory burdens) is that all net income is taxed at the corporate level, and then when it is paid out to the owners of the corporation, it will be subject to taxes again. Because of this double taxation of income it is not normally a good choice for a trading legal entity.

In order to allow people to avoid double taxation of profits another type of corporation was created: This is the **S Corporation**.

S Corporation

Although the S Corporation has a similar paperwork burden to a C Corporation, it has one significant advantage, and that is the tax treatment of income. Only income paid as a salary to the owner is subject to employment taxes, and any other income that is not paid as a salary is treated as a distribution to the owner(s) and is not subject to corporate or employment taxes.

The main disadvantages of the S Corporation include some restrictions in the way it can be operated. These include:

- No more than 75 owners
- Cannot have owners that are non-resident aliens
- Cannot have owners that are other business entities

The most significant disadvantage is in an S Corporation's inflexibility when it comes to distribution of profits. Firstly any salary paid to owners must be "a fair salary" for the kind of work that the owner does, and secondly the remaining distribution of net income must be paid in proportion to ownership in the company on an annual basis.

This is significant if you have a personal liability that means your assets are garnished, or otherwise owed to a 3rd-party. You don't have any choice about receiving the distribution of income (separate from your salary) from the S Corporation. This means it will not be protected from the personal liability. This inflexibility, and the fact that there is an increased paperwork burden for payroll processing, are the main disadvantages of an S Corporation.

Also, having to pay yourself a salary every month may give rise to a cash flow problem if your trading does not make money for a sustained period.

Limited Liability Corporation (LLC)

A Limited Liability Company (LLC) is a separate legal entity, but the paperwork burden for setup and management is much simpler than for a corporation. No board of directors is required, no minutes for meetings or resolutions, and a simple filing to maintain status (along with a tax return) is sufficient to keep the company active.

An LLC does not have the same restrictions as an S Corporation in that it can have an unlimited number of owners, and owners may be non-resident aliens or other business entities.

The main disadvantage of an LLC is that all net income (profits after expenses have been deducted) is liable for employment taxes whether it is paid out to the owners as income or not. The advantage of this however, is that the owners have total flexibility about how much and when to pay themselves a distribution from the company, and even in what percentages. This gives the owners total flexibility to make distributions as and when they like, and the accounting is done on a yearly basis rather than periodic payroll.

Basically this means that the LLC is a superior legal entity, except where your profits are very high compared to the salary you want to pay yourself. In that particular case so you could use an S corporation to avoid employment taxes on the whole net income. If you want flexibility in payment of profits, or will be paying yourself all of your net profits on a yearly basis then an LLC is a better choice in almost every way to an S Corporation.

⚖ Legal Entity Selection Criteria Summary

The table below summarizes the main differences in each of the choices based on the criteria listed.

Entity Type	Setup & Management	Liability Protection	Tax Treatment	Income Flexibility
Individual	None	None	Cannot deduct expenses	None
Sole Proprietor	Simple	None	Can deduct expenses	None
General Partnership	Simple	None	Can deduct expenses	Some
Limited Partnership	Moderate	None (for general partner)	Can deduct expenses	Some
Limited Liability Partnership	Moderate	Maximum	Can deduct expenses	Some
C Corporation	Most Complicated	If status maintained	Double Taxation	Maximum
S Corporation	Most Complicated	If status maintained	Most preferential	Some Restrictions
LLC	Moderate	Maximum	Most flexible	No restrictions

In general, if you plan to pay yourself most or all of the profits from your trading business, then an LLC is the best overall legal structure to choose. Please get professional advice tailored to your specific circumstances before making any legal entity decisions.

The table below determines the choice which relates to your most important criterion.

Your Most Important Criterion	Best Choice
Simplest Setup and Management	Individual
Liability Protection	LLC
Tax Treatment	S Corporation
Flexibility	LLC

♞ Cash Flow

Of all the problems facing a beginning trader and trading business, cash flow is the biggest and most important. How can you survive financially while your business is developing and losing money rather than making it?

As a rough guide you should assume that you will not be cash-flow-positive as a business for at least 3 years. This means that you must either have cash reserves, or alternative income, to cover all personal and business expenses for 3 years. If this means that you must continue to work for your regular employer, then that is what you must do. This is in addition to the capital you need for your actual trading account. Also, do not plan to have just enough money to last 3 years – at the end of that time is when you will want to significantly scale up your trading once you are consistently profitable, so this is not the right time to be running out of cash and having to use your trading account to live on.

If you can create the ideal situation described above, you will definitely be giving yourself the maximum chance of success. In reality, we rarely have ideal circumstances in which to develop a business and this is one of the reasons that the barriers to entry for this type of business are actually so high. Here are a few ideas on how to get closer to the ideal situation:

- **Reduce personal and business expenses to a minimum**
- **Create alternative passive income streams**
- **Send your spouse out to work**
- **Sell valuable assets to realize cash**
- **Relocate to a cheaper area**
- **Move to a cheaper house**

I did all the things listed above (apart from sending my spouse out to work) to give my business the best possible start, and chance for success, but it was still a struggle to get to cash-flow-positive. It is easy to get into the "Catch 22" situation where you cannot afford to quit your regular job, but you cannot grow your trading business if you cannot be dedicated to it full-time. In this situation I would advise spending as much time outside regular work hours working on your trading business, and saving up as much cash as you can until you have enough to see you through.

Developing alternative revenue streams (separate from your trading) is essential to the survival of your trading business. Trading income is unpredictable in the short-term. Imagine a situation where, instead of receiving a pay check at the end of the month, your employer asked for the last 2 months pay back (or the return of your bonus from last year). How would that affect your current finances? If you are relying completely on trading income then you are in for a very rough ride. Expenses are usually fixed and regular (e.g. monthly), but trading income is definitely not on a set schedule. You need other income to cover regular expenses in the months (or years) when trading is not profitable.

Some ideas for alternative income that I have implemented include:

- Providing fee-based services (e.g. financial advice)
- Teaching traders to improve their trading
- Writing and publishing electronic books and articles
- Implementing affiliate programs on pmkingtrading.com
- Writing and publishing traditional books (like this one)

The ideal situation would be that the alternative income sources are sufficient to cover all expenses and trading income is 'the icing on the cake'. Note that if you can manage to get external funds to trade, your asset management fee is an alternative (relatively) regular source of income. External funds management may be the topic of a future book but is outside the scope of this one.

Trading Systems

Although alternative income sources are important, trading should be the life-blood and main money generator for your trading business. Trading is one of the few business types that is truly scalable and you can be paid simply depending on the size of your trading account rather than the amount of work you do. The systems I trade were designed to be scalable, so it is theoretically no harder for me to trade a $100 thousand account and make $20 thousand per year, or a $100 million account and make $20 million. This was the whole reason I got into this business in the first place. At some point I will be able to employ people to actually do all the trading too and then the whole income from the trading parts of the business should become completely passive from my point of view.

It is important that you have a complementary suite of trading systems that suits your trading psychology and are not correlated with the overall markets they trade (or each other). All systems go through losing periods, but if you have a decent number of them (say 10) it is unlikely that they will all perform poorly at the same time. Also, if your position sizing and capital allocation algorithms are designed to reward winning systems and punish losing ones, you have a better chance of consistently making money overall.

It is very important that you develop a number of robust systems before starting to trade real money, and **Part II** on **Trading Management** starting on page 47 explains exactly what your system development and testing process should be to give you the best chance of success.

Operations and Management

Once you have your business plan, cash flow, and trading systems under control, it is important that you have a disciplined approach to implementing your trading systems and running your trading business.

The best way to achieve this is by keeping a journal that includes any mistakes you make, and also having various detailed checklists that you use to make sure you do everything that needs to be done on a periodic basis. I have Daily, Weekly, Monthly, Quarterly, and Yearly checklists.

⊥ Daily Checklist

An example of a simplified version of my daily checklist, primarily based on the US equity markets, which open at 9:30 Eastern Standard Time (EST) and close at 4:00 EST, is shown below:

8:00 AM	Am I "Fit To Trade"[3]
8:30 AM	Update tradable list of instruments
8:45 AM	Load historical data
9:00 AM	Check long-term system signals and positions
9:10 AM	Adjust stops on exiting positions
9:15 AM	Place orders
9:20 AM	Check for trade halts
9:45 AM	Check for short-term entry signals
10:00 AM onwards	Check intra-day signals
3:30 PM	Add to winning trades
3:50 PM	Check closing system signals
4:15 PM	Record trading errors
4:30 PM	Back-up trading environment

Having a daily operational check list helps you do everything you need to do, when you need to do it, and keeps your business running smoothly. You should have a check list for each operational "system" your business needs to run – not just your trading systems.

These operational systems include:

- Accounting
- Technology
- Tax Reporting
- Client Management
- Trading

Using online accounting and trade tracking is a good idea to minimize the operational burden on you when you have to report all your business transactions to your accountant for example.

---

[3] How to determine if you are fit to trade and what to do if you're not is covered in **Part III Trader Management**

♞ Contingency Planning

No matter how good your trading systems are, or how well you plan your trading methods, if you can't operate them accurately in a controlled environment then you will not realize the expected return from the systems as defined. In order to continuously and accurately implement your trading systems you must plan for everything that can (and does) go wrong with every aspect of your trading environment, your business, and yourself.

Listed later in this section is a "check-list" of items that may be part of your trading business (and can therefore fail at some point). Each one needs careful consideration, a backup in place (if applicable) and a written plan that states what can change, go wrong, or evolve about that particular item and what you are going to do about it when it does.

Take each item on the list (including the top-level ones) and genuinely think about how it fits into your whole operational environment and what could go wrong with it. For each contingency 'what if' list some ways of:

a) Detecting/monitoring it
b) Taking preventative or reactionary action

For example, with the item:

Trading Environment: Trading Computer: Hardware: Memory

What if a new version of a key software component requires more memory than you have in your trading PC right now? How will you continue to operate your trading systems? Can you easily revert to your backup computer with the old version of the software? Will you have additional memory at your office ready to install?

Hopefully this seems like a really big and boring task. If this is the case then it is in enough detail to actually work and prevent real errors from occurring during actual trading system operation (where an error is defined as 'I don't have a rule and plan for a situation I find myself in'). What if you don't anticipate and have rules for all feasible eventualities? You won't be able to implement your trading systems as intended and everything you do could be classed as a "mistake".

Each main section that requires contingency planning will now be discussed. The check lists are for guidelines only – your actual trading circumstances will vary, so you should think carefully about how you will manage your own trading environment if something fails.

⚖ You

Remember that you form part of your trading systems (even if you completely automate your systems and have an "auto-broker" execute them for you). You are the one who has to allocate capital, decide which broker to use (and continue using) and decide whether to change the executing system or any of the decisions you have made that went into creating the implementation of the system. There are various points of failure with you as part of your trading business. These are dealt with in much more detail in **Part III** on **Trader Management** starting on page 152.

> Physical State
> Mental State
> Availability
> Motivation

⚖ Your Trading Environment

The quality and effectiveness of the environment within which you operate your trading business is a key to success. If you have ever tried to accurately trade a system with a 4-year-old running around you will know exactly what I mean. Every aspect of your trading environment must be made the best it can possibly be and you should have backups put in place for all unforeseen circumstances you can think of.

> Power
> Lighting
> Ergonomics
> > Noise
> > Smell
> > Temperature Control
> > > Heating
> > > Cooling
> > Comfort
> Phone Line
> Cell Phone
> Accessibility
> Security
> > Physical (i.e. theft, protection from elements)
> > Technological (i.e. hackers/viruses)
> > Intellectual Property

37

1 Your Trading Technology

Almost all trading businesses rely on some kind of technology today. Even if you draw all your charts by hand, you must get your prices from somewhere, and have a way to send orders to your broker. Yes, I know you can phone orders in, but who does that anymore?   The telephone is technology too.

Trading Computer
    Hardware
        Screen
        Mouse
        Keyboard
        Processor
        Power
        Router
        Modem
        Microphone
        Speakers
        Backup Device
        Hard Drive
        Memory

    Software
        Operating system
        Web Browser
        Email Client
        Broker Software
            Account
                Capital
                Positions
                Margin
                Voluntary Corporate Actions[4]
                Withdrawals
                Deposits
        Trading System Software
            Trading System Code
            Bugs/defects
            Erroneous executions
            Version control
            Quote software (historical and real time)
            Other Data Services
            Symbol Information

---

[4] Convertible bond conversions, early option exercises, etc.

```
                Involuntary Corporate actions
                        Splits
                        Mergers and Acquisitions
                        Bankruptcy
                Backup Service
                Virus Protection
                Firewall
```

```
Internet Service
        Internet Service Provider
                Email server
                Internet gateway
                Call center
        Internet connection
                Cable
                Digital Subscriber Line
                Dialup
                        Landline
                        Cell phone
                Wireless
```

ı Your Trading Systems

The main cash-machine part of your business is your trading systems and you must have contingency rules in place that allow you to detect and react to problems with your systems. This is covered in much more detail in **Part II** of this book, **Trading System Management** which starts on page 45.

```
Trading System
        Research
        Development
        Testing
        Implementation
        Operation
        Performance (both good and bad)
Suspension and Resumption
Monitoring
Capital Allocation
Scalability
Retirement
```

Your Trading Venues

Whatever your actual trading methods are, there must always be some way for you to actually implement your trading ideas by buying and selling a financial instrument. The venues you choose for your trade implementation are keys to your success. What is the point of having an excellent trading system if you can't accurately and quickly implement the orders it generates? Contingency planning for what to do if you can't enter a trade (or much worse, exit an existing position) when you want to is very important to avoid those huge losers that can wipe out many months of trading profits in only a few moments.

Broker
    Account
        Statements
        Stops
        Order Execution
        Dividends
    Exchange Linkage
    Trading Software Server/Connection
    Call center
    Commissions and Fees
    Bankruptcy/Liability

Exchange
    Trade Halts
    Regulatory Change
    Delisting
    Fees

Other Market Participants
    Specialists
    Market Makers
    Dealers

⚖ Your Business Environment

Changes in the operating environment of your business can seriously affect your overall profitability and it is important you have rules in place to identify, detect, and react to significant changes in your operating environment. Protecting yourself from liability issues, regulatory changes that can affect the validity of your trading systems, and general business operational rules is something that should be a very detailed section of your business plan.

Regulators
- Tax Rules
- Legal Issues
- Registration Requirements
- System Idea/Hypothesis Implications
- Margin Rules
- Fees

Trading Business Entity
- Liability
- Legal
- Regulatory Requirements
- Tax Issues
- Accounting
- Cash Flow
- Balance Sheet
- Capital Requirements
- Other Business Participants
  - Attorney
  - Compliance Officer
  - Trader
  - Administrative Assistant
  - Accountant
  - Technology Manager

♟ Other Factors

Other factors that are part of your overall business (and therefore need contingency planning) but are not included specifically in the other sections of the contingency report are shown below.

> Clients
> Family
> Friends
> Expectation Management (what to do if you don't meet your expectations)
> Other Legal Issues
> Other Liability Issues

Your contingency plan should form a big part of your overall operation planning work. There is a very good reason why franchised businesses succeed far more often than non-franchised business – and the answer is in the planning. A franchise has built-in manuals for operating the business in a proven way, including contingency planning about what can go wrong and how to fix and react to it. This significantly increases your chances for success and a trading business is no different than other businesses – if you plan for all eventualities you will have a much better chance of succeeding.

♟ Professional Advice

No business can function without the help and support of a specialized team of advisors. This includes attorney, tax advisor, accountant, trading coach, and financial advisor. As a minimum I would recommend a good attorney (you will need them to help set up the legal entity for you) and an accountant (you do not want to be doing your own tax returns – you want to concentrate on trading and running your business effectively).

You may think that professional advice is a luxury that your new business cannot afford, but it would be a false economy – one simple mistake on a tax return, or misreporting trading income could cost you much more than retaining the professional services would have done.

Always seek referrals from people you trust for professional advice even if you study a particular subject and consider yourself a well-informed client.

♞ Business Management Summary

Note that having completed your business plan, your work is not finished – the plan needs to be updated regularly as your circumstances change and your business grows and develops. You should create a periodic task that says "Update business plan" at least yearly. I find myself updating it almost weekly as I work through the tasks I have set myself as a result of the business plan.

It doesn't have to be a formal document under version control either – in fact having a more flexible "journal style" approach with periodic updates to the main plan is a much better idea since it is supposed to be a working document that helps you run your business, not a "constitution" that has to go through layers of bureaucracy to be changed.

If you find you can't or won't find the time to write a formal plan for your business, I would take it as a very clear sign that building a trading business is not suitable for you. Keep looking until you find something you are passionate enough about to actually make the effort to write the plan for.

A common cliché in the trading business is:

"Plan your trade, trade your plan".

This applies just as much to the whole business level as to an individual position. Operating without a complete plan at any time is a costly mistake since your results are going to be due mainly to luck rather than skill (or hard work).

⅄ Part I Critical Success Factors

Having a complete, detailed, and realistic business plan is the first (and actually most important) step in developing a trading business. If you have a written plan your chances of success go up significantly.

Planning your trading business should involve detailed work on each of the following areas:

- Objectives
- Legal Entity Selection
- Contingency Planning
- Operational Management
- Cash Flow

Don't start risking your cash (or quitting your current job) until you have a complete and detailed plan.

A change is as good as a rest

Summer 2003, Fair Haven, New Jersey

The business has been running for over a year now. Severance and health insurance from my previous job has stopped but the huge monthly expenses haven't. My son is 15 months old. I don't know how to trade well yet and things are hard.

Cash flow is killing me; every month our cash reserves get less, expenses seems to be getting bigger, and our "crunch point" gets closer and closer. We decide to leave Fair Haven; why pay for the expense of living right next to a major city if I'm not working there? We want to live somewhere more rural. All the business needs is a high-speed internet connection and to be in Eastern Standard Time.

We sell our house and move to Vermont. We can't find a property we want to buy, so everything we own, apart from what will fit in the car, is left in storage in New Jersey until we buy a house. We hope to find something suitable in the next couple of months. It actually takes over a year to find what we're looking for.

I get an office in Middlebury. We rent a cabin up in the mountains in Ripton where the seclusion is fantastic (we never got Moose in the garden in Fair Haven!) but it seems like the winter lasts 6 months of the year. It takes 10 minutes just to get down the forest road to Ripton, and another 25 minutes to my office on a good day. Oh well, I can't work from home – the phone service is flakey, cell phone service is non-existent, and no chance of high-speed internet.

All our expenses seem to be bigger than we anticipated (although nothing like they were in New Jersey). I concentrate on becoming a good trader. That seems to be the most important thing right now. If I can learn to consistently make money everything will turn out all right (I hope).

Part II – The Middle Game: Trading Management

Trading systems are the "life blood" of the business; if your trading isn't profitable you don't really have a trading business.

As I have mentioned previously, trading systems are the life-blood of your trading business and are the thing that will ultimately turn your business into a scalable money-making machine.

Making money by trading requires only 3 things to be true:

1. You have a funded trading account
2. You have a complete, positive expectancy trading system or method
3. You accurately implement each trade your system generates

The previous section on **Business Management** covered what is required to ensure item 1 above. This part of the book is about Item 2 – how to develop a trading system or method that should make money. The next part on **Trader Management** starting on page 152, completes the picture by explaining how to consistently achieve Item 3.

Because it is impossible for you to consistently and accurately implement a trading system that is not specifically suited to your own trading personality, it is recommended that you do not actually trade any systems you have developed until you have read and understood both the sections on **Trading System Management** and **Trader Management**. If you must trade before then, due to an uncontrollable need to lose money, please trade as small as possible. Also, this is the main reason that buying a trading system is very unlikely to result in profitable trading. Failure is much more likely if you haven't achieved these three keys to success:

a) Matched your trading systems specifically to your personality
b) Come up with the idea for the trading system yourself
c) Gone through the rigorous development and testing process personally

The chances of the system working for you are remote if you don't have all three. It is very likely that you will abandon it after a losing period.

This part of the book tells you everything you need to know to develop your own trading systems starting with an idea, all the way through to implementation and trading with a full allocation of your trading capital.

♟ Trading System Development

The keys to effective system development are firstly an understanding of the contribution made by each component of a trading system (in terms of the trait or behavior of the system), and secondly how these relate to your overall objectives.

In this section I deal with the main system objectives:

- Implementation Costs
- Risk & Reward
- Expectancy

How they relate to each main system trait:

- Commission
- Slippage
- Trade Frequency
- Cash Made
- Risk of Ruin
- Win Percentage
- Average Winner Size
- Average Loser Size
- Average Trade Duration

How each system component determines the overall personality of the system:

- Market & Instrument Type
- Instrument Filter
- Setup & Entry
- Position Sizing
- Exit Strategy

If you clearly understand how each component of your system affects the system's behavior or performance, you have a much better chance of developing systems that exactly meet your objectives.

♟ The Model

The trading system component model diagram (**Figure 1** below) shows a representation of the Objectives, Traits and Components of a trading system. Each section of the model will now be described briefly, and then in detail in later sections.

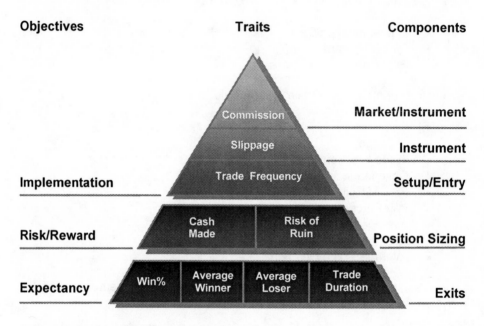

Figure 1: The Trading System Component Model

♟ Trading System Model Aspects

Objectives form the foundation of why we trade. In order to perform effective system development we must always know what the objectives for our trading system are. The objectives for a trading system are split into 3 main areas:

Implementation Costs	– spread, slippage, commission, interest payments, cost of carry, etc.
Risk & Reward	– expected return and maximum drawdown per time period
Expectancy	– average amount made per unit risk

Traits are descriptions of specific behaviors of a trading system. These characteristics determine whether the system is suitable for your personality or not. System traits include:

Commission	– how much you pay for entering and exiting a trade
Slippage	– the difference in price of your actual entry to your anticipated entry
Trade Frequency	– the number of trades per period
Cash Made	– the absolute amount of cash you make
Risk of Ruin	– your chances of a drawdown that would mean you would suspend trading
Win Percentage	– how often you have winning (and therefore losing) trades
Average Winner Size	– the average size of your winning trade
Average Loser Size	– the average size of your losing trades
Average Trade Duration	– the average length of your trades

Lastly the trading system itself has **Components** that are primarily responsible for each system trait – it is this relationship that is the key to developing, testing and improving your trading systems.

System components include:

Market & Instrument Type	– what markets you are trading, and which instrument types (equities, options, fixed income, foreign exchange, etc.)
Instrument Filter	– which instruments in the chosen market you consider liquid and volatile enough to trade
Setup & Entry	– what conditions determine a trade is possible and should be entered
Position Sizing	– how big each position should be for the life of the trade
Exit Strategy	– when to exit winning and losing trades

Each main aspect – Objectives, Traits, and Components will now be covered in more detail.

♟ Trading Objectives

One of the keys to successful trading is to be sure to define your objectives before attempting to develop a trading system. For example, you could say you want to make 20% per year return and are prepared to suffer a 20% draw down in initial capital. As with any interesting and challenging activity, knowing what you are actually trying to achieve plays a big part in how you go about achieving it.

The objectives for a trading system (beyond actually making money obviously) can be split into 3 main areas:

Implementation Costs	– which we want to minimize
Risk & Reward	– which need to be balanced from a psychological comfort level point of view.
Expectancy	– which needs to be positive to give us the trading edge we desire

Each aspect will now be discussed.

♟ Implementation Costs

Most traders just accept implementation costs as a necessary evil of trading, but they are actually one part of your system that can be designed to your requirements to some extent. The main implementation costs include:

Commission which is dependent on the instrument type you choose to trade coupled with the broker you choose to execute your trades.

Spread and **slippage** are both dependent on how liquid the instruments you select are compared to your desired position-size. Having instrument filters that only trade the most liquid instruments can significantly reduce spread and slippage.

Other implementation costs include dividends on short equity positions, margin interest, cost of carry for foreign exchange trades, and rollover for futures contracts. Each of these must be carefully considered relative to the expected return of the system to ensure they are not going to negate any positive return generated by the system This is far more significant for trading systems that are high-frequency and short-term, but not so much of a problem for longer term systems.

⏚ Risk & Reward

Decisions that need to be made *before* you commence system development include:

- Risk - how much of your trading capital you are prepared to lose
- Reward - how much reward per period you are expecting to realize

Any system (that makes money on average) can be designed to achieve a specific risk and reward profile by choosing an appropriate position-sizing algorithm. Position-sizing is like the volume control on your hi-fi – it doesn't actually change the music playing (your core system) but have it set too loud (too much risk per position) and you get distortion (you will exceed your risk parameters and may blow up your account) or too low (not enough risk per position) and you will not be able to hear the music (you will not achieve your expected reward).

⏚ Expectancy

Expectancy is the amount of reward (on a per-unit-risked basis) your system makes on average. It is defined simply as the average of the profit or loss per unit risk (based on your initial stop) per trade.

For example, if you have a trade where you made $2000, but would have lost $1000, based on where your initial stop was, that would be a reward:risk ratio of 2:1. This value is commonly referred to as **R**, and this trade would be a 2R winner. The initial risk is always represented by a positive number, the profit as a positive number, and any loss as a negative number.

Expectancy in this context is simply the average **R** for all the trades a system takes. If this value is below zero you have a negative expectancy system and you should not trade it.

Systems can be designed to achieve a positive expectancy primarily by creating effective exits that focus on generating average winners that are much bigger than average losers. This de-emphasizes your winning percent (and in fact creates a situation when the win% at which you will break even with your trading is less than 50%). This means you don't need to be right more often than chance to still make money. Exits are covered in detail in the section called **The Importance of Exits** on page 72.

Having clearly defined goals for each of the previously described objectives *before* commencing system development will put you in a much better situation to make rational decisions about how your system development and testing is progressing.

♟ System Traits

Traits of a trading system are specific behaviors that can be directly manipulated or determined by decisions you make when developing a system. They describe the overall personality of the trading system and determine exactly how it meets your objectives.

♟ Commission

Commission is the cost of buying and selling something, charged by your broker, and is completely under your control according to which broker you choose. For some instrument types (e.g. foreign exchange) the commission is 'hidden' in the spread, so is not a separately reported item. Minimizing commission is one of the easiest ways to increase the expectancy of your system – especially for high frequency trading systems.

♟ Slippage

Slippage is the difference in actual price to expected price and is usually negative (i.e. actual price ends up higher than expected on a buy order, and lower on a sell). Slippage can be reduced by only choosing to trade the most liquid (i.e. highest volume) instruments that trade in the most orderly way. Remember that slippage happens both on entry and exit of a trade so it is important to monitor the liquidity of an instrument during a trade and exit before it drops to an unacceptable level if possible. Sometimes volatility changes are too rapid to react to and you simply have to rely on your exit strategy to get you out of trades where volatility or volume is no longer favorable. Also, slippage can be a large proportion of your overall trading cost – again, especially for high frequency trading systems.

♟ Trade Frequency

Trade frequency is determined by the sensitivity of your setup (rules that signal a potential trade) and entry (rules that actually get you into a position). It is important to remember that average trade frequency is directly under your control, but that any setup/entry will go through periods of more and less trades. There is usually a tendency to get a clustering by order side if you trade both long and short – i.e. you will tend to get clusters of long trades followed by clusters of short trades rather than a mix of both at the same time. This clustering of trades is generally unavoidable but you should have rules in place that determine how you will select between potential trades if you get too many for your available capital. Having an ordering preference based on one of the variables in your setup rules is a simple way of doing this.

⚖ Cash Made

The ultimate objective of trading is to make money by selling something for more than you paid for it (or vice versa if you trade on the short side). If this is not the primary objective for your trading you may be in serious trouble when exposed to the rigors of trading your system for real. The absolute amount of cash (in base currency units) any system makes is dependant on the position-sizing algorithm and how you allocate capital to the system. Reward is always proportional to risk, but for any given system it is the position-sizing algorithm that determines your overall reward. This is clearly demonstrated in the section starting on page 86 called **The Importance of Position Sizing.**

⚖ Risk of Ruin

Since reward always goes hand-in-hand with risk it is not possible to have a position-sizing algorithm that achieves a certain reward without generally taking approximately the same amount of risk. Therefore it is the position-sizing that determines what your chances of hitting your maximum drawdown are (which is a good definition of risk of ruin – rather than a total loss of capital). The more you "crank up" your expected reward, the more risk you are taking per trade, and the bigger the draw-down will be when you hit a string of losers.

⚖ Win Percentage

Win percentage – how often you get to be right – is one of the least important aspects of a trading system. It is also the one that is least controllable, unless you trade some short-term anomalous pattern that your system has been curve-fit to detect; which is not recommended. All robust, long-term winning systems tend to make most of their money from having average winners much larger than average losers, thus de-emphasizing winning percentage. For example, if you have average winners one and a half times as big as average losers, then you can have 40% winning trades and still break even (i.e. not lose any money).

This is a much better situation to be in than relying on a system that has to be right a lot to make money. Even so, trading lower winning percentage systems is psychologically difficult to do for most traders who tend to equate winning trades with being right (or a good trader) and losing trades with being wrong (or a bad trader).

♪ Average Winner Size

This is where the money is made in trading – generating large winning trades and riding them as far as they will go. Exits that are generous to winning trades (i.e. wider stops for winners), that only tighten when further chance of large profits are diminished should be used to make winners as large as possible. Obviously for winners to get big, you must trade instruments where the price moves enough. Trading only higher volatility instruments is important (which is part of your instrument filter criteria). Again, letting profits run is psychologically difficult to do for most traders since there is a tendency to take profits too early for fear they will slip away.

♪ Average Loser Size

This is where risk is reduced to a minimum in trading – keeping losers small and stopping them before they grow too big. Exits that are harsh on losers (i.e. tighter stops), that never widen and tighten quickly when a position is inactive should be used to make losers as small as possible. Obviously for losers to stay small you must always, always stick to your exit strategy and exit a loser at the first opportunity rather than let it get big. Cutting losers short is psychologically difficult to do for most traders since there is a tendency to hope the loser will turn around and become a big winner.

♪ Average Trade Duration

The average length of time you are in a trade is determined by how far your initial stops are away from your entry price relative to the underlying volatility of the instrument you are trading. Because of this, your average trade duration is mostly under your control and an exit strategy should be chosen that gives you an average trade length that is matched to your setup/entry frequency. You don't want to be generating few trades which you exit quickly, or many trades which you stay in too long – neither situation is efficient usage of your capital.

♟ System Components

Putting this all together, it is now time to specifically relate the system traits to the main components of a trading system and describe interdependencies between them. This allows you to target the development and redesign of each system component in the context of the traits it affects, and therefore the objectives for your trading system it supports.

Market & Instrument Type

When choosing a market and instrument type, your decisions should primarily be oriented around how to minimize commission for the instrument type you want to trade by selecting the lowest cost execution venue or broker.

Instrument Filter

Instrument filter should be concerned with finding the most liquid instruments within your chosen market. This should minimize spread and slippage and help to create the lowest-cost implementation environment for your system. Selecting higher volatility instruments will also increase the chance of hitting a big winning trade.

Setup & Entry

Setup and entry should be designed to create trades at the desired frequency at times where there is the most chance for a move in your chosen instrument. Note that this has nothing to do with predicting the future direction of an instrument or the chance of a winning trade – that is determined by your exit strategy. It is impossible to tell in advance which trades will be the winners or losers so we simply want a setup and entry that is designed to get us in at a time when a good move is likely at the desired trade frequency.

Position Sizing

Given any positive-expectancy system, position-sizing can be used to match the variability of return expected from the system to your desired risk and reward objectives. Simulation of the variability of returns can be invaluable in choosing an appropriate position-sizing strategy for a given system and is covered in the section starting on page 105 called **The Importance of Simulation.**

Exit Strategy

Exit strategy is the primary component of any trading system because it encompasses most of the important traits of your system including average winner size, average loser size, winning percentage, losing percentage, and average trade duration. For this reason the majority of your system development effort should be focused on good exits that seek to implement the age-old trading cliché of 'Cut your losers short and let your winners run'. This is covered in **The Importance of Exits** starting on page 72.

♨ Trading System Model Summary

The trading system model previously presented forms the foundation of thinking about how to go about developing trading systems, so it is important that you understand how it fits together before attempting system development.

You should understand how objectives must be decided in advance. Objectives include what implementation costs will be, how much risk you are willing to take for any given reward, and how much actual cash you are willing to risk.

You must understand how traits (the ways your systems behave) impact objectives and include commission, slippage, trade frequency, cash made, risk of ruin, win percentage, average winner size, average loser size, and average trade duration - and also how they are determined by each system component.

System components (the building blocks of your system) include market and instrument type, instrument filter, setup and entry, position sizing, and exit strategy and you need to consider how each component relates to each system trait.

By my nature I am a logical, consistent, systematic, analytical, and disciplined thinker, so treating trading as a system came naturally to me. There are huge benefits to having a set of rules that dictate what to trade, when to trade it, how much to trade, and when to exit your positions. Therefore, the following sections are what are required to implement a complete systematic approach to trading. I appreciate that some traders are purely discretionary, but to me that means they simply have a discretionary entry signal. All the rest of the trading system development material is still applicable even if you exercise discretion over what to trade, and when to trade it.

The main advantages of having a trading system are that it can be tested to see if it would have made money historically, it can be selectively optimized to meet your requirements under different circumstances, you can identify markets in which it performs well and poorly. Performance testing also allows you to differentiate losing money because of the system itself and from your accurate, or poor, implementation of it. With purely discretionary trading you are the system, so it is difficult to separate the system from the trader.

With systematic trading all the work, research, and development is done up-front, and this leaves maximum effort left over to actually implement the system accurately with minimal discretionary input when it comes time to trade. It also means that you have a pre-defined rule for every eventuality during the trading day and should never find yourself having to make a critical decision on the spur of the moment under pressure.

♟ The Trading System Lifecycle

A trading system goes through a lifecycle from inception to retirement, and each phase of the life of a trading system must be carefully monitored. The development phases of a system are:

1. Idea
2. Hypothesis
3. Research
4. Development
5. Historical Testing
6. Real-time testing
7. Small real money testing
8. Optimization
9. Full Capital Allocation
10. Monitoring
11. Suspension
12. Retirement

Each phase in the life of a trading system will now be described. Please refer to **Figure 2** on page 59 which outlines the first phase of the process of trading system development from Idea (number 1 above) to the completion of Historical Testing (number 5 above).

First, I will discuss the process of system development, then the individual components of a trading system. Finally, the lifecycle of a trading system within the context of your trading business will be covered.

Idea

Every trading system starts with an idea. The idea is a concept that describes some aspect of the way a particular market, or all markets, work. Ideas come from reading trading books, magazines, trading web sites, or just observing the markets on a daily basis. For a trading system to be successful it must be based on an idea that you truly believe and have researched yourself. Some areas for research that I have found interesting include:

- Gaps at the opening of trading indicate a severe order imbalance between buyers and sellers and have recurring patterns.

- The close of trading is an artificial and arbitrary point in time. Prices do not cease to move simply because the market is closed.

- Companies that buy back their own stock are reducing supply so if the laws of supply and demand apply to stocks, the price should rise.

Whatever areas interest you, ideas should have some foundation in reality, make sense, and occur with a frequency that is useful and can be tested.

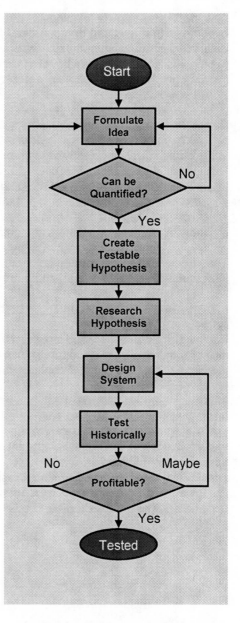

Figure 2: Trading System Development – Testing Phase

1 Hypothesis

The next step in developing a trading system is defining a testable hypothesis that is based on your idea. It must be possible to find supporting data to test your hypothesis, and you must be able to quantify the hypothesis so that it can be programmed and tested. The market and instruments that the hypothesis is applicable to should also be included. An example would be:

Since the close is an arbitrary halt in trading, instruments that have exhibited significant intra-day swings in a particular direction should continue to move in the same direction on subsequent trading sessions.

In order to quantify this rule we must have precise definitions for each of the variable in our hypothesis. In the example this means we have to define which markets we are talking about, which instrument within each market, and how big a move constitutes a 'significant' move in a particular direction.

The quantification of your hypothesis gives rise to the market selection, instrument filter, setup signal, and entry signal for your system.

In our example we might come up with the following rules:

For all US Equities Traded on the NASDAQ that have more than a X% increase in price from the open to Y minutes before the close, enter long at the close if they are within Z cents of their high for the day.

This represents a testable hypothesis that we can turn into a mechanical trading system in order to test whether it would have been historically profitable and created enough trades to be a useful trading system. Note that at this point in the development of our trading system we have not specified exact values for the variables in our hypothesis (X, Y and Z) – that comes later after we have done our research into the viability of the system. Also, we have no definition for the most important parts of the system: The exit strategy (when to get out) and position-sizing (how big to trade).

Research

Having specified a testable hypothesis, and identified the variables that define the trading system we can research the viability of the system. I strongly suggest that you do this using a computer and automate the testing process. Researching a hypothesis manually is time consuming, tedious, and also prone to psychological errors since we always want the system to succeed in order to prove how clever we are. In fact, your research should be biased towards disproving the hypothesis, since a lot of promising ideas result in trading systems that are no better than random, or produce too few or too many trades for your requirements.

In order to research our example we would need data that gives us the Open and Closing Price of all NASDAQ listed equities, and the Open, High, Low, and Close of the following few days to see how effective our entry signal is in the period immediately following the signal. Not that we are looking for movement in the price – not necessarily in the correct direction, just some indication that this is a good time to enter a trade.

At this point we can calculate the percentage change each day, and choose a number that gives us a reasonable amount of trades based on our requirements. For example if we want one trade per day, choose a percentage move that happens at least once per trading day.

I use a spreadsheet program and a product that retrieves historical quotes using the internet so I can easily and quickly test any hypothesis. Various trading system testing environments exist that do 80% of the work for you automatically, but in my experience it is the last 20% that they can't do that is the important stuff. Taking the time to learn how to test your own trading systems is very important and could be the main thing that gives you the confidence not to abandon your systems when they go through an (inevitable) losing period.

Development

Once we have the idea, hypothesis, variables, and data we need we can develop the system in a testing environment to see if it has any value. First a filter must be designed that only includes the specific market(s) and instruments(s) defined by the hypothesis.

Then we can build a list of each trade that would have been signaled by the system, and finally apply some position sizing and exit criteria to see whether the system would have made money overall.

At this point we will simply use 'sensible' values for the main variables in the system rather than trying to choose the values that yield the most profit (i.e. optimization). This avoids "curve fitting" our system to past data that will result in a system that looks great historically but is unlikely to be successful in the future during real trading.

1 Historical Testing

Each aspect of the system can be tested individually to make sure it performs to requirements, before testing the whole system. Specifically we can have multiple instances of the same system designed to test each aspect individually:

1. Entry Signal + fixed position size + fixed exit signal
2. Entry Signal + fixed position size + variable exit signal
3. Entry Signal + variable position size + variable exit signal
4. Entry Signal + variable position size + variable exit signal + implementation costs

In test 1 we would only trade 1 round lot or contract, and exit after a fixed time period (e.g. at the close 5 days from entry). The chosen time period should be representative of the average trade length we are looking for in the finished system.

In test 2 we would introduce a profit-taking or trailing stop that would allow profits to run on longer for trades that are big winners.

In test 3 we would position-size as a percentage of capital allocated to the system, based on previous trades so that as the system wins it can risk more, and position size is reduced during a losing streak.

In test 4 we would include a calculation for commissions and estimations for how much the entry and exit price would differ from the historical prices in our test data (i.e. slippage). This last test is important because it identifies systems that are profitable, but not enough to overcome the cost of implementing them. This is most common in high frequency (i.e. intra-day) trading systems and you may need to adjust trade frequency and average trade duration to achieve a positive result.

The diagram on page 63 represents the rest of the trading system development process from testing in real time to allocation of capital. This will now be discussed.

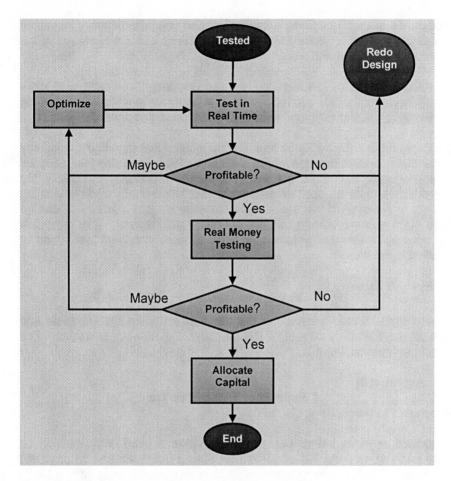

Figure 3: Trading System Development – Implementation Phase

♪ Expectancy

At this point we must go into more detail about defining a way of comparing the different instances of the trading system. A good way of doing this is called system expectancy. For each trade the system makes we calculate the ratio of Profit or Loss to Initial Risk (as a positive number); this can be referred to as R. Then take the average R to calculate Expectancy (E).

Expectancy gives us a measure of how much this system should make on average per unit risk. For example if you are risking $1000 on a trade (based on the size times the difference in the entry price and your estimated stop price) and the expectancy of the system is 0.25, you should make $250 per trade on average.

Expectancy is useful because it can be used to compare different instances of a single system, or completely different systems since it is always in the same units (profit per unit risk).

So, using expectancy in each case we can compare the results, and know exactly how much of the profit (or loss) is attributable to which aspect of the system (entry, sizing, exit, commissions, or slippage and spread).

Obviously if the expectancy is negative (or goes down significantly) for any of the tests (except the one where implementation costs are included) we have a system that does not work, or needs modification. Ideally the expectancy should be positive after each test. Note that when risk-limiting aspects of the system are added (such as stop losses) expectancy can go down since you are limiting risk and therefore also reward. This is normal and does not mean the system is no good or the component just added or modified is not useful.

ⵑ System Value

A more sophisticated measure of the value of a trading system takes into account the variability of results (R) and also the number of trades. The formula for system value is:

$$\frac{\textbf{Average(R)}}{\textbf{Standard Deviation(R)}} * \textbf{Number of Trades Per Year}$$

A modified or simplified version of system value is used in the section on **Exits** (starting on page 72) and **Position Sizing** (page starting on page 86) to compare different trading systems. Note that in order for system value to be comparable the number of trades must be annualized (or standardized to some constant time period) for each system.

If the system has positive expectancy overall, after trading costs are factored in, then it is worth moving on to the next stage which is testing in real-time on paper. If the system has negative expectancy we can choose to abandon it, modify it, or attempt to optimize the variables to make it work. In my experience optimization of a negative expectancy system should only be considered if it is *only* the trading costs that are causing the system to lose money – not the system itself. Optimization in this case is used to reduce the trade frequency and increase the average trade duration in order to reduce trading costs to manageable levels.

At this stage 'informal' optimization can be used by changing each of the variables in the system to see how they affect overall expectancy. The system should be positive expectancy over a large selection of values for the main variables in order to consider it a "robust" system. If the system only works with a few specific values for the main variables then it is likely to be a short-term anomaly and will not work for a reasonable period of time. Systems that exhibit this behavior should be abandoned.

One other aspect to be wary of is a very high win percentage. If the system has winning trades more than about 60% of the time it is also likely to be a short-term anomaly and will fail in the near future. Alternatively this could be due to exits that take profits too early and let losers run – which is the opposite of what you want to do. How will you be able to predict when the anomaly possibly switches around (usually overnight) to a 40% winning system instead?

Assuming the system performs well over a number of years that exhibit all the different market types (see next section, **Market Types**) we can fix the main variables at a value that yields the desired number of trades. Once we have a "frozen" version of the system we can then move on to real-time paper trading it. Calculating the expectancy of the system for each market type is a good idea at this point since it tells us how robust the system is with respect to market. This will be an indication of whether we will be able to trade it full-time, or have to temporarily suspend it in certain types of market.

♟ Market Types

Most trading systems are affected by the overall market conditions of the markets they trade. Robust systems will make money in nearly all types of market, but will make more in some types of market than others.   For example, most trend following systems are especially vulnerable to many small losses when the markets they trade are moving sideways without any distinct trend.

Note that market type classification is not predictive – it simply states what kind of market we are in right now.   In my experience it is generally impossible to predict changes in market type in any way that is useful to our trading.

This section details a systematic way to classify the current market environment based on trend and volatility, and gives a way to test the performance of your trading systems to see if they are vulnerable to changes in the prevailing market environment. This allows us to only trade a system when market conditions are currently favorable, and either reduce or eliminate the capital allocation to a system when market conditions are unfavorable.

A particular market can be classified in 2 ways:

Volatility (Low, Normal, and High)
Trend (Up, Down, and Sideways)

These 2 classifications can be combined to give us 9 different possible types of market:

	Volatility	Trend	Market Type
1	Low	Down	LD
2	Low	Sideways	LS
3	Low	Up	LU
4	Normal	Down	ND
5	Normal	Sideways	NS
6	Normal	Up	NU
7	High	Down	HD
8	High	Sideways	HS
9	High	Up	HU

Methods for classifying a market into Low, Normal, and High Volatility, and Up, Down and Sideways Trend will now be discussed, as well as how the market type can be used to manage your trading systems effectively.

♟ Market Volatility

Market volatility is about how much the price of an index or other representation of a market moves about over a particular time period. Some normal level of movement is desirable since most trading systems can only make money if prices are in motion. Individual instruments exhibit their own volatility, but it is the overall volatility of the market to which they belong that we are concerned about for our market classification.

Firstly we must define what constitutes 'the market' for each of the instruments our trading systems trade. For a US Equity System we could use all equities on all the major exchanges (i.e. the New York Stock Exchange, the NASDAQ, the AMEX), or we could use an index such as the S&P 500 as a 'proxy' for the overall market. If you have a list of equities your systems consider tradable, you could use this as a proprietary index, and base market volatility calculations on it.

If there is no suitable proxy, or the market or exchange on which the instrument trades is very distinct from the instrument itself (for example commodity futures), then the actual instrument can be used to calculate a volatility measure.

As an example we will take US Equities, and use the S&P 500 as the representation of the market in which they trade. The next step is to determine how we will measure the volatility of our market proxy (S&P 500).

There are 2 main ways to calculate the volatility of a market:

- Based on price movement of the market or individual instruments
- Based on implied volatility of options on the market proxy or instruments

Note that we are only concerned with current volatility relative to historical volatility in order to assess whether a market is exhibiting volatility that is lower, the same as, or higher than normal; the actual volatility measurement is not that important as long as we apply it consistently.

For the S&P 500 example we could use the daily price range (High-Low) over the last 10 days as a percentage of the index value if we wanted a price-movement-based volatility measure.

We could also use the VIX as a representation of implied volatility for the S&P 500 index options. Since the VIX data is readily available this is an easy way to measure the volatility of the S&P 500 in this case.

Once we have chosen our volatility measure we need to calculate it historically and then define a way to classify current volatility as below, the same as, or above what is normal. An effective way to do this is to use the Standard Deviation. Standard Deviation is a measure of how widely a value is distributed around the average of all values. In our case we could say that if current volatility is within 1.5 standard deviations of average then it is 'Normal'. If current volatility is greater than 1.5 standard deviations from average then volatility is 'High', and if current volatility is less than 1.5 standard deviations from average then volatility is 'Low'.

Now we have a way to calculate and classify the market volatility, we can have a similar process for the current trend of the market.

Market Trend

The second component of our market classification is the current trend. This is basically whether the market's price is moving up, down, or within a sideways range. A simple way to determine trend is to take a simple moving average of the price and then calculate the slope of the line. If the slope of the simple moving average is above a certain threshold then the trend is up, if it is below a certain threshold then it is down, and in all other cases it is considered a sideways trend.

Another way is to calculate a short-term moving average and a longer one. When the short term one crossed the longer one it represents a change of trend. It is important to choose a period to calculate your moving averages that reacts quickly enough to changes in trend so that your market classification is a representation of recent activity, not too far in the past. This is especially true if your trading system has a short timeframe (e.g. a few days). The trend calculation should always be calculated over a similar period as the holding period of the trading system you are testing.

If you have various trading systems that trade over different holding periods, you can always split your trend classification into Short, Medium, and Long Trend, and then use the trend classification that is relevant to the system being tested.

A Market Type Example

As an example, **Figure 4** on page 69 shows the S&P500 Index classified into the 9 different market types over the last 10 years. To measure the volatility I used an ATR over 30 days and then calculated this as a percentage of the closing price of the index.

For trend I calculated the slope of a SMA of the close over 30 days. In both cases I used a standard deviation to determine the bands for "low", "normal", and "high" with a value within 1 standard deviation of average representing a "normal" volatility and a "sideways" trend.

As you can see from this example the market classification spends a lot of time in Market Type 5 which is a "Normal volatility sideways trending" market. Also over the last 10 years the market classification has never been Type 1 which is a "Low volatility down trending" market. These two observations are to be expected since:

a) Markets do not trend all the time, and
b) Down trending markets are generally characterized by higher rather than lower volatility.

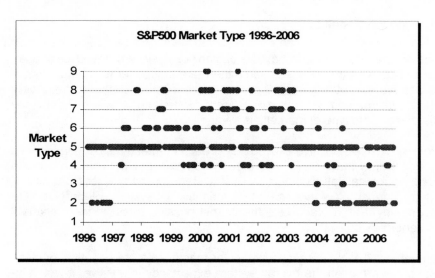

Figure 4: S&P 500 Market Classification, 1996-2006

The length of the averages used in the market classification calculations should be adapted to the average trade duration of your systems. The daily trend and volatility over the last 30 days is not relevant if your average trade durations are measured in minutes or months.

⚐ Trading Systems and Market Type

The most basic way to use market type is to measure how our system performs within each market classification. To do this we need a measure of a system's performance we can compare across market types. System Expectancy is a useful way to achieve this.

Expectancy is useful because it can be used to compare the performance of a system in each market type since it is always in the same units (Profit per unit risk).

So, calculating expectancy for each type of market that the system has traded in directly shows us the effect of the overall market on our system performance. Note that it is important to calculate the number of trades that were used to calculate the expectancy for each of the 9 market types. If there are less than 30 trades in any particular expectancy calculation, then that result will not be statistically significant and can be ignored until more trades are generated (either by real trading in the future or hypothetical simulated trades using historical data from further in the past).

⒤ Using the Results

Once we have our expectancy calculation for a system based on market type, we can use the results to see if there are any patterns. If your system has positive expectancy in all 9 market types – congratulations, it is a very robust system, and you can have confidence that it will make money regardless of the type of market it is trading in.

If your system has positive expectancy in each market type, but certain ones are significantly lower than the overall system expectancy, you can use this to reduce the capital allocation to your system for the market types where performance is below average. This means your system will be given the most money to trade (and take the largest position sizes) in the markets it has performed best in.

If any of the expectancies for a particular market type are negative, or close to zero, even though the overall system expectancy is positive, it would be an indication that your system does not perform well during these types of market. A simple solution is to suspend trading of the system when the market conditions are unfavorable. It is common for trend-following systems to perform poorly during high volatility, sideways (HS) market types, and it may be desirable to temporarily suspend trading them during this type of market.

Always be aware, however, that any kind of suspension of a positive-expectancy system may simply result in lowering your overall profits by "missing" trades that are signaled as a market goes from one type to another. The only way to "guarantee" every trade will be made is to keep trading the system (at some size) regardless of market type.

Market Type Summary

In this section we have detailed a way to classify a market based on volatility and trend, and then described how we can calculate the performance of a system based on the market type.

In this way we can be sure we are only trading a particular system when market conditions are favorable, and suspend trading when it is less likely to make money.

The 9 different market types:

1. Low volatility downtrend
2. Low volatility sideways trend
3. Low volatility uptrend
4. Normal volatility downtrend
5. Normal volatility sideways trend
6. Normal volatility uptrend
7. High volatility downtrend
8. High volatility sideways trend
9. High volatility uptrend

So far everything has been about finding trades to enter successfully. Although entry is important when considering trade frequency, it is the exit strategy (when to get out of positions) that determines the average size of winners versus losers, the overall winning percentage and therefore the expectancy of the system. The next section discusses exits in detail and how they affect overall system performance.

♟ The Importance of Exits

If I had to list one thing that is misunderstood most often when developing trading systems it would be how exits affect overall system performance. Almost every trader I know has fallen into the "trading trap" of trying to maximize profits by searching for a "highly accurate" entry signal at one time or another. This is a futile exercise since, as this section will demonstrate, winning percentage is determined by your exit strategy, not your entry.

In this section we discuss the 4 main types of exit:

1. Discretionary
2. Inactivity
3. Risk Management
4. Profit Taking

With examples from a simple trend following system I will demonstrate how, just by changing the exit strategy, a system's performance can be adjusted to suit your personality, objectives and requirements.

The 6 systems we analyze are all based on the S&P 500 index and coded in TradeStation®:

System 1 – Basic entry with fixed time exit
System 2 – A high winning percentage exit
System 3 – A low winning percentage exit
System 4 – An inactivity exit
System 5 – An additional risk management exit
System 6 – An additional profit protection exit

The historical hypothetical results from TradeStation® of each system will be compared to see how the exit strategy affects the overall performance of the system. Please note that the examples use historical data, and a theoretical index that can't be directly traded. The results are for explanatory purposes only and should not be interpreted as actually achievable in real life trading.

♈ Discretionary Exits

Although this book is primarily concerned with mechanical or systematic exit strategies we must first discuss situations where positions should be closed for other reasons. These are discretionary exits and include the examples below.

These exit rules are about anything that should or could cause you to exit a position (or all positions) that are not due to one of the other types of systematic exit rules covered later. Discretionary exit rules may be at one of two levels:

- System Level
- Position Level

Each will now be discussed.

♈ System Level

Examples of system level discretionary exits where you close some or all of the positions for an entire trading system include:

- You are unable to monitor your system for new entries, or manage existing positions for a period of time.

- You have some environmental problems (technical, physical, ergonomic etc.) that mean you are not trading in an optimal environment.

- You are going through a personally stressful time, or doing something that means you cannot give the required attention to your trading that the system was designed to need.

- Your technical trading environment (computer, internet connection, backups, other hardware or software) that your system is dependent on is not functioning as intended.

- You have met or exceeded your parameters for maximum drawdown.

- Your system is operating outside of any 'normal parameters'. (This may include excessive profits as well as losses). This will be covered in more detail in the section **The Importance of Simulation** starting on page 105.

- You get too many entries for your available capital and cannot take any more positions.

⚴ Position Level

These are specific unpredictable events that may cause you to exit a position immediately which are not directly price-based like the other types of systematic exit.

Examples of this type of discretionary exit include:

- Liquidity dries up in the equity for some reason (i.e. it is no longer on your list of tradable instruments).

- A company has been purchased by another entity (or taken private i.e. it is no longer a public company). This one could be considered a mandatory exit if you wait until the company is de-listed.

- You get a new entry that has better risk/reward than this position (i.e. the current position is a loser) and don't have the available capital to keep this position and enter the new one.

Discretionary exits are designed to reduce errors by not trading when you have less chance of accurate implementation. Even though they are not systematic, it is still important to have rules in place that determine exactly how you will implement them accurately and consistently. Thinking of, analyzing, and writing down formal procedures for discretionary exits is a useful exercise and a section in your business plan should be dedicated to this.

The other three main types of exits are all to do with price. These are:

- Inactivity Exits
- Risk Management Exits
- Profit Taking Exits

These will now be discussed.

↟ Inactivity Exits

If a position is range-bound for a pre-defined period of time, it means you are taking risk in the position but receiving no reward. This position should be exited so that your capital may be allocated to a 'better' risk/reward opportunity. This is especially important if you are trading a system that can take multiple simultaneous positions, or you are trading multiple systems in the same account. Efficient use of your capital on only the "best" risk/reward positions is essential. You should not have "dead money" for long periods in positions that are going nowhere.

For example, the length of the period you consider to be significant should be proportional to average trade duration and have some kind of threshold for the profit or loss you would consider a "non-performing" trade. This should normally be proportional to the volatility of the instrument you are trading (i.e. a high-volatility instrument may have a bigger "non-performing" threshold). Using the R-multiple for the trade is a good way to allow you to have a non-performing threshold that is comparable across systems (even with different time frames).

You could choose ±0.5R as your non-performing threshold, or ±0.25R. Generally you want your definition of "non-performing" to be a fraction of the initial risk (R) rather than something that approaches 1R.

↟ Risk Management Exits

These rules are often called 'stop loss' rules. Getting rid of losing trades within your pre-determined risk parameters is a very important type of exit. These exit points should be:

- Normally based on price only
- Outside the 'normal noise' of the instrument (i.e. be volatility-based)
- At a point that clearly says 'the setup has failed, this is *unlikely* to become a winning trade'

Note that the actual amount of risk you are taking with a particular exit is determined by your position-size in combination with your exit price. Always remember that sometimes it may not be possible to exit within the parameters set by your stop (on a gap at the open for example). For this reason your initial risk is always only an estimate of what loss you could actually incur. You could have greater than 1R losers due to severe market moves (which are unavoidable), or implementation errors where you don't stick to your system (which are usually preventable). This is covered in the section called **Implementation Errors** on page 143.

Generally these kinds of stops should not be loosened, only tightened, even if volatility increases after you enter the position. This is the embodiment of the common (but useful) trading cliché:

CUT YOUR LOSSES SHORT

This is what keeps your average losing trade smaller than your average winner, which is a big contributing factor to a positive expectancy system.

⅄ Profit Taking Exits

These exit rules are for positions that are in profit only. These exit points should be:

- Normally based on price only
- Outside the 'normal noise' of the instrument (i.e. be volatility-based)
- At a point that clearly says 'the trade has given me all it is likely to and the chance of further profit is clearly diminished'

Generally these types of exit points should trail from your entry, and may be loosened if volatility increases to give winners more 'room to breathe'. This is the embodiment of the common (but useful) trading cliché:

LET YOUR PROFITS RUN

A simple volatility-based (e.g. a multiple of the Average True Range over some recent historical time period) stop trailed from the high/low or close is very effective.

Note that any particular position can (and often does) switch from winning to losing and vice versa. This simply means that the exit rules that are currently in force for the position may change over time. It is simple to spot a loser from a winner. If the current R value of the trade (including implementation costs) is positive it's a winner, if it's not then it's a loser.

Generally having pre-defined price targets is not effective unless your setup includes something that can determine the likely extent of a winning trade. Profit-targets are usually an example of 'cut your profits short' and are generally counter-productive since they actually reduce the average size of a winning trade. This will be demonstrated later in this section when we compare different exit strategies for systems with an identical entry.

Profit taking stops should be designed to keep your average winning trade large (compared to your average loser) which is a big contributing factor to a positive expectancy system overall.

⅄ Other Factors

Generally it is a bad idea to have a rule that attempts to move your stop to breakeven as soon as possible. This is a psychologically comfortable thing to do, is arbitrarily based on your entry price, and is therefore common to everyone trading a similar system/setup to you who has a similar entry point. Therefore, it is often the case that a position returns to your entry point after a few days simply because lots of 'breakeven stops' have been placed there. All breakeven stops are then hit before the market then moves on to where it was going in the first place.

Since most exit rules are price-based, you should always view the last price as the 'real price' regardless of how much or little volume there was at that particular price. You should be trading liquid instruments specifically so that you have an orderly market in the instruments you trade so you should never believe a price is a 'bad tick', 'anomaly', or 'market manipulation' and therefore always *stick to your exits accordingly* based on the current price.

⅄ System Comparisons

The systems used for our example are all based on a basic trend-following entry that trades both long and short in the S&P 500 Index. Since this is a theoretical instrument for demonstration purposes, it cannot be traded in real life, but all the TradeStation® code for each system is included at the end of this book in case you want to reproduce the results, or apply them to an instrument you can actually trade. The systems do not take more than one position at a time.

In our testing sample weekly bars going back 10 years were used.

⅄ The Entry

The basic system has an entry that is the bar's closing price crossing above or below the 12 bar simple moving average (SMA) of the close.

- Go long if the close crosses the SMA(12) from below.

- Go short if the close crosses the SMA(12) from above.

This is one of the simplest entries possible, so we know all our system traits and characteristics really come from the way we change the exit strategy – not from anything to do with having a sophisticated, complicated, over-optimized, or anomalous pattern entry.

This is not meant to be a profitable or rational entry that we recommend for your trading, but simply one to give us a reasonable frequency of trades to see the effect of our exit strategies whilst keeping the entry criteria exactly the same for each sample system.

⚖ System Value

In order to compare each instance of a trading system as we change and add exit strategies we will use an adaptation of the **System Value** described on page 64 for each instance. Since we are using fixed position-sizing and a theoretical instrument we will adapt the System Value formula to our requirements.

System Value is a relative measure of performance that combines profit (or loss) per unit risk, the variability of profits and losses and the number of trades per period. Since we are not using stops for most of our demonstration systems, we do not have an initial risk estimate, and therefore we don't have a quantified initial risk. For this reason we will use the simplified formula below:

$$\frac{\textbf{Average(Profit or Loss in Points)}}{\textbf{Standard Deviation(Profit or Loss in Points)}} * \textbf{Number of Trades in Testing Period}$$

Additional data that is useful for comparison purposes is the average size of winners compared to losers, the winning and losing percentage, and the number of trades per year. Note that although we are using exactly the same entry in all cases, the number of trade may change due to the way the system exits positions and can therefore take new ones. These attributes are included in the data table for each system.

⚖ Comparison Attributes

Attributes we care about for each test system are listed below:

Win%	– How many winning trades the system makes
Average Winner Size	– Average size of winning trades to compare to average loser size
Average Loser Size	– Average size of losing trades
Number of Trades	– Total "round trip" trades over the testing period
Points Profit	– Whether the system makes any profit overall not including implementation costs (e.g. commission, slippage, etc.)

The TradeStation® code for each system is listed at the end of this book for your information. If you want the actual EasyLanguage® code please use the "Contact Us" page at www.pmkingtrading.com.

⚖ System 1 – Fixed Exit

System 1 is our "control" system which uses the simple moving average crossover entry previously described. The exit is fixed at 12 bars (which is 12 weeks in this case). This forms the baseline for our comparisons since it has no other exit strategies.

System Value	Number of Trades	Win%	Lose%	Average Winner	Average Loser	Points Profit
1.67	21	52%	48%	61.52	-54.18	134.99

Since there are no price-based exits, this system basically takes unlimited risk from the entry to the fixed time exit – price could theoretically go anywhere and we would not exit. The points profit is therefore misleading because we are taking virtually unlimited risk. Also, the average size of winners is not much bigger than losers which means we must rely on a higher winning percentage to make money. Since the winning percentage will tend towards 50% (i.e. random) for an arbitrary fixed exit, this system is of little real value.

⚖ System 2 - A high win% exit

System 2 is a demonstration of how a high winning percentage can be achieved simply by changing the exits. This system exits after 1 bar if the trade is a winner. It also has a 100 bar fixed exit for practical reasons to finally exit large long-term losing positions.

System Value	Number of Trades	Win%	Lose%	Average Winner	Average Loser	Points Profit
0.73	22	77%	23%	17.10	-249.13	41.50

This system's winner versus loser size is much worse since we are taking profits immediately, but letting losses mount – this is the opposite of "Cut losses short, let profits run". Even though the higher winning percentage is psychologically comforting (since we get to be right a lot – 77% of the time), the actual profit is worse than in System 1 since all the small winners are wiped out by the big losers. System value is below 1 which indicates a much poorer system in this case.

⅄ System 3 - A low win% exit

System 3 is a demonstration of how a low winning percentage can be achieved simply by changing the exits. This system exits after 1 bar if the trade is a loser. It also has a 100 bar fixed exit for practical reasons to finally exit long-term winning positions.

System Value	Number of Trades	Win%	Lose%	Average Winner	Average Loser	Points Profit
-7.67	44	5%	95%	311.42	-28.99	-594.60

Although the average winner is now way bigger than the average loser, this system's winning percentage is low enough to completely wipe out that advantage. The number of trades has also gone up (and with it the implementation costs if you actually traded this system) since losers are exited quickly so new signals can be taken. Taking losses quickly is a good thing to do, but in this case we do not have a way of protecting the profit from winning trades, so the moment they turn from winners to losers they are exited and the profit slips away. The System Value in this case is indicative of a system that consistently loses (a lot of) money.

⅄ System 4 - An additional inactivity exit

System 4 has an inactivity exit that closes trades after 6 bars if there is less than 10 points profit or loss. This exit attempts to close "non-performing" trades so that capital can be used for new entries. In this case we used a simple "number of points" definition for inactivity since we have no initial stop loss and therefore can't calculate an R multiple for the trade to use as a measure of inactivity.

System Value	Number of Trades	Win%	Lose%	Average Winner	Average Loser	Points Profit
0.75	24	46%	54%	43.23	-38.68	49.90

This is the first system with a "sensible" exit strategy that exits "non-performing" trades to free up capital for subsequent signals. The average winner is now bigger than the average loser, and the system generates a modest profit. The system value is below 1, but positive again. A more sophisticated approach would be to have a volatility-based measure of "non performance", both in time and price that adapted to changes in volatility rather than using fixed parameters.

ᴣ System 5 - An additional risk management exit

System 5 has an additional risk management exit which is a simple stop based on the Average True Range over the last 12 bars. This exit attempts to limit the size of losing trades i.e. cutting losses short. It also has a 100 bar fixed exit for practical reasons to finally remove large long-term winning positions.

System Value	Number of Trades	Win%	Lose%	Average Winner	Average Loser	Points Profit
-1.47	14	36%	64%	84.33	-70.55	-213.32

This system has a stop loss that is effectively reducing risk therefore some big winners (that at some point were large losers) are no longer included. This is why the system value has gone down. Average winner is still larger than the average loser, but the overall loss is bigger due to the decreased winning percentage. The number of trades has dropped because some trades that were exited at fixed intervals before are allowed to stay open as long as they are within the risk management stop. This is an example where an exit reduces system performance because it is (sensible and necessarily) reducing risk. System Value is now negative since risk has been limited but profits are still not protected.

ᴣ System 6 - An additional profit protection exit

System 6 has an additional profit protection trailing stop which simply trails from the highest high (for longs) or lowest low (for shorts) once a certain profit target is reached. This exit attempts to protect some open profits from winning trades whilst giving them "room to breathe" i.e. letting profits run.

System Value	Number of Trades	Win%	Lose%	Average Winner	Average Loser	Points Profit
1.49	26	62%	38%	38.67	-47.80	140.74

Average winner size is still not greater than average loser size, but the system is now profitable, and the results are less volatile. This is because the exits are working in concert to:

- Exit inactive positions
- Limit the size of losers
- Protect the profit on some big winners

81

The profit protection exit should be refined in conjunction with the other exits to create a system where average winner is greater than average loser. This would also increase the System Value.

⚖ System Comparison Summary

System Number	System Value	Number of Trades	Win%	Lose%	Average Winner	Average Loser	Points Profit
1	1.67	21	52%	48%	61.52	-54.18	134.99
2	0.73	22	77%	23%	17.10	-249.13	41.50
3	-7.67	44	5%	95%	311.42	-28.99	-594.60
4	0.75	24	46%	54%	43.23	-38.68	49.90
5	-1.47	14	36%	64%	84.33	-70.55	-213.32
6	1.49	26	62%	38%	38.67	-47.80	140.74

As we can see from the system value score for each system, the one with the complete set of exits (**System 6**) has the best overall profit and a system value almost as good as System 1, which has no exits to manage risk or protect profits. The equity curves (in points) generated by each of the systems are shown starting on page 83.

⌁ Positive System Value Equity Curves in Points

The chart below shows the simulated historical equity curves in cumulative points profit or loss for the systems that have a positive system value:

- System 1 – Basic entry with fixed time exit
- System 2 – A high winning percentage exit
- System 4 – An inactivity exit
- System 6 – An additional profit protection exit

As you can see, each exit strategy produces different results with exactly the same entry. **System 6** is only "under water" at the start and has the least volatile equity curve overall.

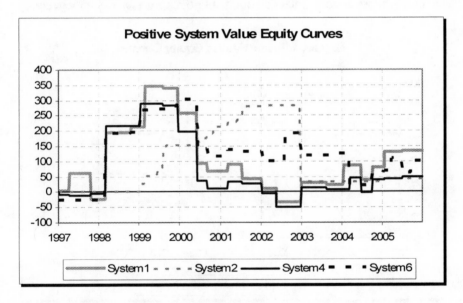

Figure 5: Exit Strategies Positive Value Equity Curves

⅄ Negative System Value Equity Curves in Points

The chart below shows the simulated historical equity curves in cumulative points profit or loss for the systems that have a negative system value:

- System 3 – A low winning percentage exit
- System 5 – An additional risk management exit

The two systems that have negative end results (even though the trades for the original default entry have positive expectancy overall) are **System 3** (low win percentage) and **System 5** (just risk management but no profit protection). System 3 simply takes all losers straight away, so is an example of not taking enough risk to make a reasonable return. System 5, with no profit protection, limits risk but does not capture profits effectively.

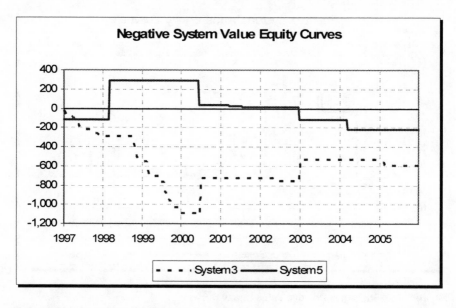

Figure 6: Exit Strategies Negative Value Equity Curves

♨ Exits Summary

Each system using the same instrument and entry was historically tested with different exit criteria to observe the effect on overall performance. The conclusion was that the system that had superior overall performance and risk management was the system (System 6) that had a complete, but simple, set of exit criteria including:

- Inactivity Exits
- Risk Management Exits
- Profit Protection Exits

As you can see from the system results, exits are what determine the main performance characteristics of a system. Exits can be used to create high winning and losing percentages. Each system exhibits completely different characteristics even though the instrument traded, testing period, and entry criteria are identical in each case.

Consequently the majority of your system development effort should be focused on exits and not on the other parts of a trading system.

After exits, the thing that makes the most difference to performance, and the only thing that matches your system to your objectives is how big each trade should be (for its entire life from entry to exit). This is your position-sizing strategy and is the topic of the next section.

♟ The Importance of Position Sizing

Position-sizing strategies answer the question "how big" a position to take from the start of the trade at the entry, all through the life of the trade until you exit the position. Position-sizing is like the volume control on your music CD player – it can't actually change the music (the underlying system), but if you have it turned up too loud you will get distortion (blow up your account) and too low you won't be able to hear the music (won't meet your objectives).

Position-sizing is the bridge from the core expectancy of your trading system to meeting your objectives for risk and reward. Obviously position-sizing cannot make a negative expectancy trading system make money in the long-run, so you need to develop and test a complete, positive-expectancy trading system that suits your personality and requirements before you even consider what good position-sizing looks like.

It is a good idea to test a system with single lots or contracts and reasonable estimates for commission and slippage in your chosen market to ensure the system has positive expectancy before attempting to apply position sizing strategies.

In this section we discuss the 6 main types of position-sizing strategies:

- Fixed Size
- Martingale
- Fixed Dollar Amount
- Fixed Percent
- Averaging Down
- Scaling In

In this section we will use examples from the simple trend following system (**System 6**) we developed in the previous section on exits on page 81. We will demonstrate how, just by changing the position-sizing strategy, the system's performance can be adjusted to suit your particular objectives and requirements. Each strategy will generate exactly the same set of trades – only the position-sizes are different.

The 6 systems we analyze are again all based on the S&P 500 and coded in TradeStation®:

System 6 – Trades 1 unit per trade
System 7 – Doubles the trade size after a loser (Martingale strategy)
System 8 – Risks a fixed dollar amount per trade
System 9 – Risks a fixed percentage of account value per trade
System 10 – Adds to losing trades (averaging down)
System 11 – Adds to winning trades (scaling in)

The historical hypothetical results from TradeStation® of each system will be compared to see how the position-sizing algorithm affects the overall performance of the system.

♟ Position-Sizing Strategies Discussed

The practical implications of each of the main types of position-sizing strategy will now be discussed.

If you have a negative expectancy trading system (i.e. the reward per unit risk is negative) then position-sizing can only change the duration of how long it takes to lose all your money. Basically, you should avoid trading if your system has a negative expectancy. The optimum strategy if you do decide to play a negative expectancy game (or system) is to bet everything you are ever going to bet on one trade. This minimizes the effects of the negative expectancy since you are participating for the shortest amount of time possible (apart from avoiding playing at all).

Since longevity is the key to successful trading, it is always preferable to trade a positive-expectancy system with reasonable position-sizing that meets your objectives. The rest of the discussion in this section assumes that you are using a positive-expectancy system. It discusses and demonstrates how different position-sizing techniques affect the overall results even though each system is generating exactly the same set of trades.

Fixed Size

The basic system (**System 6**) that was developed in the section on exits, on page 81, will be used as the core system with which to test the different position sizing-algorithms.

System 6 has the following characteristics:

- Trades the S&P 500 index on historical weekly bars going back 10 years
- Can take long and short positions
- Enters long when the close crosses above the Simple Moving Average (SMA) of the close over 12 bars
- Enters short when the close crosses above the Simple Moving Average (SMA) of the close over 12 bars
- Has an inactivity exit
- Has a volatility-based risk management stop based on the Average True Range (ATR)
- Has a volatility-based profit protection trailing stop based on the Average True Range (ATR)

The position-sizing algorithm in this case is to trade 1 unit (share or contract) per trade. This is the base-line system that we can use as a comparison for each of the other position-sizing strategies.

Martingale

Martingale position-sizing is a technique where the size of positions is doubled after a loss. The etymology of this technique is somewhat obscure, but one plausible explanation is that it is named after Martigues, in the Provence region of France. Roulette was supposedly popular there in the 18th Century and people liked to use a strategy where they started off with a one unit bet, and doubled the bet size after each loser. This position-sizing algorithm "guarantees" that you will win 1 unit assuming you do not run out of money before you get a winner, and the house allows you to scale up your bets to the desired size.

In practice, roulette is a negative expectancy game since the payout is 50:50 on Red and Black (for example) but the Zero (or sometimes also Double Zero) on the wheel are neither red nor black. This means that the odds of Red or Black are less than the 50:50 payout, therefore the game has negative expectancy. Another undesirable feature of this technique is the fact that your reward:risk ratio quickly becomes psychologically undesirable after only a few losers.

With roulette it is perfectly plausible to have, say, 8 losers in a row. If you started off betting one unit, after only 8 losers in a row, you would have to bet 256 units on the next spin of the wheel (having already lost 255 units) to end up winning 1 unit overall. This is obviously not a good reward:risk ratio. Generally any strategy that increases size after losing is counter-productive and will be psychologically difficult to follow through with. Even assuming you don't run out of cash before you give up.

ᴚ Fixed Dollar Amount

The next type of position-sizing described is risking a fixed dollar amount per trade. This does not mean if you want to risk $10,000 then you should buy $10,000 of an instrument because the actual risk you are taking is the difference between your estimated entry price and your "worse-case" estimated stop price, multiplied by your position size. The whole position is not at risk unless you have a stop at zero. For instance, if you trade options, and decide that the whole option premium is at risk. This means that you will not attempt to exit if the premium goes down to a certain point – you will just let the options expire worthless and take a total loss.

For example, if you are going to buy an equity priced at $100, and your risk management stop is at $80, then you are taking $20 per share risk, so in order to risk $10,000 you would purchase:

$10,000 / ($100-$80) = $10,000 / $20 = 500 shares

Note that this particular strategy does not take into account whether the system has won or lost money in the past – the risk remains the same ($10,000 per trade) regardless of your actual account value. The only decision you have to make is how much risk per trade you want to take. If you calculate that your system will generally have a maximum of 10 losers in a row and you don't want to lose more than $50,000 then you can select a per-trade risk of:

$50,000/10 = $5,000

The main drawback of this system is that it does not vary position size based on how much your account has in it, or whether a system is winning or losing at the moment.

₤ Fixed Percent

In a fixed-percent model the position-size is proportional to your current account value. This means that position will get smaller if the system loses, and larger if the system wins (which is basically the opposite of a Martingale strategy and why this technique is sometimes called an Anti-Martingale strategy).

For example, if you wanted to risk 1% of account equity per trade and your account size was $1,000,000 then 1% would be $10,000. The position size would be the same as in the previously discussed fixed dollar amount algorithm. However, as the system won or lost money, 1% of the current account size would change. So, for example, if the account had gone up to $1,500,000 then 1% would be $15,000 risk so the number of shares (with the stops and price the same as in the previous example) would be:

$15,000 / ($100-$80) = $15,000 / $20 = 750 shares

As the account value goes up and down, the position-sizes would increase and decrease. This has a tendency to have progressively larger positions when the system has a winning streak and progressively smaller ones as the system loses money. Unlike the fixed dollar position-sizing it is not actually possible to lose your entire account with fixed percentage position-sizing since you are always risking less than 100% of the remaining capital. This does not mean you cannot hit your definition of "ruin" which is the point at which you would stop trading due to losses. Also, if you have trades that are greater than -1R losers, due to implementation errors, or other problems, you could also lose your entire account.

Obviously if you set the percentage risk too high, this method can actually be more risky than the fixed dollar amount. For this strategy you have 2 main decisions:

- What percentage risk should you use?
- What calculation should you use for current account value?

The percentage risk you should use should be based on the probable maximum number of losing trades you expect to experience along with your tolerance for draw-downs. Simulation of the variability of returns of your system is a good technique for determining this and is covered in the section starting on page 105, called **The Importance of Simulation**.

The second decision is what current account value you should use for the calculation. Your main choices are:

- Current Net Liquidation Value
- Current Cash
- Estimated Value if all your stops on your current positions are hit

Current Net Liquidation Value

In this calculation one simply takes the current net liquidation value of the account (including all cash and the value of open positions) as the value upon which to calculate position sizes. It is optional whether you include commission and slippage in your calculations. Note that for futures contracts (that are "marked-to-market" in real time) this value represents what your account would be worth if all positions were closed right now at the market so it does include open profits or losses in futures positions. This is, however, the simplest calculation because it is reported by your broker (usually in real time for electronic brokers since they have to perform near-real-time margin calculations).

Current Cash

In this calculation one simply uses unused cash as the account value to size new positions on. This is the most conservative choice since generally the actual amount of risk you are taking is less than the actual value of your positions (except for futures contracts which have no actual cash value). This calculation results in the smallest position-sizes for new trades.

Estimated Value

The last alternative is to value your account as if each position was stopped out at the current stop price, and position-size on the amount of cash you would have in your account if all positions were closed. This is a reasonable compromise and is the truest indicator of your current actual level of risk in open positions. This is a value you should be calculating for your account anyway to see what your actual level of risk is across all systems and positions so it should not be much additional work to use it for position-sizing purposes. This measure is commonly referred to as "portfolio heat".

Another more sophisticated technique is to use one percentage of some notion of "core capital" plus another percentage of open profits. Periodically "resetting" your account to 100% "core capital" is a good idea if you use this technique. This means that the proportion of risk to core capital and open profits does not become unbalanced over time as your system hopefully makes money. Resetting open profits to core capital on a fractional basis over time is also possible.

Averaging Down

Averaging down is a technique that increases position-sizing for losing trades. This is psychologically comfortable to do using the reasoning that "it was a good price when I entered, it must be a great price now". The main drawback, however, is that it guarantees that you will have your biggest positions on your worst losing trades (and if you don't set a limit on adding units you could lose your entire account). For this reason I don't generally recommend adding to a losing position under any circumstances. If trades are either winners or losers, and we can't tell in advance which they are going to be, why would you "bet" more on a loser turning into a winner – isn't it already saying "I'm a loser" loud and clear?

Scaling In

Scaling in is a technique that only puts on a fraction of a "full" position at the start of the trade, and waits until the trade turns into a winner before "scaling up" to a full position. This helps ensure that we have the biggest positions when we have winners (although at a higher average cost) and smallest positions on losers. Although this technique generally reduces overall actual profit, it can have the effect of "smoothing" the equity curve. Another advantage is that it allows very large positions (relative to the daily volume of the traded instrument) to be "split" into parts to minimize market impact or slippage. This is applicable to institutional or proprietary traders trading very large size (or if you are trading illiquid instruments - which is not recommended anyway. Your instrument filter should already have selected only the most liquid instruments in your chosen market).

The main drawbacks of scaling-in are that big winners will have smaller position-sizes to start with (and higher average cost) and that reduces returns. Additionally, trades that start out as winners (so you scale in) and then turn into losers will actually lose more than if you had stuck to one unit position sizes from the start. Generally these disadvantages are offset by the smoother equity curve, but this depends on your own objectives for total reward compared to your tolerance to the emotional pain of a possible "rollercoaster" equity curve.

⚐ Other Methods

Position-sizing algorithms that seek to optimize only total return to the detriment of other considerations (such as equity-curve volatility, risk of ruin, and emotional trading "pain") include:

The Kelly Criteria

A betting strategy based on information theory that generally attempts to size so one has an x% chance of a (1-x)% loss. For example, using Kelly Criteria we could position-size to attempt to have only a 1% chance of a 99% loss (based on estimated odds for each possible outcome). This strategy is best suited to fixed-odd or known probability systems such as horse-racing or sports betting rather than the variable odds and unknown probabilities of trading.

See William Poundstone's excellent book "Fortune's Formula" reviewed in the "Reading" section of pmkingtrading.com for more information on this particular method.

Optimal F

Optimal F is another strategy that is designed to maximize return from a system but makes the (poor) assumption that one's worse drawdown is in the past. This generally greatly exaggerates the "reasonable" percentage that should be bet on each trade and dangerously increases one's real chances of ruin. This strategy is therefore not included in my definition of practical position-sizing techniques.

One explanation for why one's biggest drawdown is always in the future is that if we assume for a moment that trading system returns are random, then like the common "random walk" of drunken men example (explained in Poundstone's book previously mentioned) the average distance from the starting point of an entire crowd of drunken men moving at random is proportional to the square-root of time.

Since the number of trades for a trading system is also proportional to time, then it would follow that the distance from your starting point (i.e. starting account value) is also proportional to time. Thus it would follow that the biggest absolute drawdown is always in the future since "distance from starting point" is increasing with the length of time the system has been traded for.

The practical result is that Optimal F:

- Is based on the assumption that we only care about maximizing return.
- Is based on the assumption that maximum future drawdown is the same as the past.
- Usually ends up with position-sizes that most experienced traders would consider hyper-aggressive.
- Increases your risk of ruin to unacceptable proportions with virtually any trading system except one that never has any losing trades.

My advice is to steer clear of this particular sizing algorithm - therefore none of the systems in the examples that follow actually use it. Try increasing the fixed percentage trading system (**System 9**) example to, say, 30% risk per trade if you want some indication of what effect Optimal F has on overall equity curve volatility.

♟ System Comparisons

The systems used for our example are all based on the basic trend-following entry that trades both long and short in the S&P 500 Index. Since this is a theoretical instrument for demonstration purposes, it cannot be traded in real life, but all the TradeStation® code for each system is included at the end of this book so you can reproduce the results or apply the systems to different time periods and instruments. For simplicity, the systems do not take more than one position at a time.

In our testing sample we used weekly bars going back 10 years.

♟ The Entry

The basic system has an entry that is the bar's closing price crossing above or below the 12 bar simple moving average (SMA) of the close.

- Go long if the close crosses the SMA(12) from below.

- Go short if the close crosses the SMA(12) from above.

This is about as simple an entry as one can create, so we know all our system traits and characteristics come from the way we change the position-sizing strategy – not from anything to do with having a sophisticated entry criteria.

♟ The Exits

The system has the 3 main types of systematic exits:

- Inactivity
- Risk Management
- Profit Protection

The inactivity exit closes out positions that have not moved significantly in a certain number of bars.

The risk management exit is a simple volatility-based (ATR) stop.

The Profit Protection exit is an ATR-based trailing stop that is incorporated after a trade reaches a certain profit threshold.

This is not meant to be a profitable or rational system that we recommend for your trading, but simply one to give us a reasonable frequency of trades.

This allows us to see the effects of our position-sizing strategies whilst keeping the whole "core" system (and therefore the trades it generates) identical for each sample system.

₰ System Value

In order to compare each instance of a trading system as we change the position-sizing algorithm we will use an adaptation of the **System Value**. Since we are using a fixed core system and a theoretical instrument we will adapt the System Value formula to our requirements.

System Value is a relative measure of performance that combines profit (or loss) per unit risk, the variability of profits and losses and the number of trades per period. Since we are not changing the core system (and therefore the trades for each one are identical) for most of our demonstration systems, the number of trades the system takes in these examples are identical. For this reason we will use the simplified formula below:

$$\frac{\text{Average(Profit or Loss in Points)}}{\text{Standard Deviation(Profit or Loss in Points)}} * 100$$

Additional data that is useful for comparison purposes is the average size of winners compared to losers and the maximum drawdown (in points) that the system generates because that can actually be affected by the position-sizing algorithm even when it operates on exactly the same set of trades. Note that due to this different calculation, the system values shown in this section should not be directly compared with those in the section on exits.

₰ Comparison Attributes

Attributes we care about for each test system are listed below:

Maximum Point Profit	– The maximum value the equity curve reaches
Minimum Points Profit	– The minimum value the equity curve reaches
Winning Percentage	– This should not change during the course of the test
Average Winner Size	– Average size of winning trades to compare to average loser size
Average Loser Size	– Average size of losing trades
Points Profit	– Whether the system makes any profit overall not including implementation costs. (e.g. commission, slippage, etc.)

The TradeStation® code for each system is listed at the end of this book.

System 6 – Fixed Size

System 6 is our "control" system which is the simple but complete system previously described. This forms the baseline for our comparisons since it has a fixed "1 unit per trade" position-sizing algorithm.

Note that the results for this system test are not identical to the result for exactly the same system code in the section on exits since a slightly different historical time period was used. Also, if you have read the TradingSpotlight™ Article, "The Main Caveats of Back Testing" available from www.pmkingtrading.com, you will already know that getting identical results running tests at different times is virtually impossible because of data changes and fixes going on in the background you don't get to see.

System Value	Maximum Points	Minimum Points	Win%	Average Winner	Average Loser	Points Profit
7.97	303.05	-162.15	62%	38.67	47.80	140.74

Since there is actually no position-sizing algorithm, this version of the system simply makes a return in direct proportion to the number of points profit generated. Increasing the number of units traded would simply increase the profit (and drawdown) in proportion. Position-sizing is not altering the behavior of the system at all (or therefore the actual System Value).

System 7 - Martingale

System 7 is a demonstration of how a Martingale (doubling after a loser) strategy would work. The system starts off with 1 unit and then doubles the position-size after a losing trade. After a winning trade the position size returns to 1 unit again.

System Value	Maximum Points	Minimum Points	Win%	Average Winner	Average Loser	Points Profit
20.49	448.22	-29.86	62%	61.83	54.11	448.22

As you can see, this really increases the profit and the system value, and reduces the drawdown. On the surface this looks like an ideal position-sizing strategy. Unfortunately it does not take into account the possible maximum number of losing trades. With a 38% losing percentage, having 10 losers in a row is actually quite likely (try tossing a coin 100 times and see how many tails you can get in a row). If you used this strategy and did have 10, 54.11 point (average loser size) losers in a row you would lose over 55,000 points. Now do you think it is still a good position-sizing strategy to use?

⚖ System 8 – Fixed Dollar

System 8 is a system that takes a fixed dollar amount of risk per trade. Using a "contract" value of $50 per point, this system sizes positions to risk $10,000 per trade (based on the initial stop).

System Value	Maximum Points	Minimum Points	Win%	Average Winner	Average Loser	Points Profit
0.97	277.73	-134.82	62%	46.85	-72.79	21.66

As we can see the system value has gone way down, and the average loser is now much greater than the average winner. The total points profit is small even though the minimum points is not much higher than in System 6. This shows that a fixed dollar position-sizing strategy does not adapt well to the sequence of winners and losers for a system and actually makes the overall return characteristics worse. This type of strategy is not recommended.

⚖ System 9 – Fixed Percentage

System 9 risks 1.5% of the current net account value (starting at $100,000) based on the initial stop. Because this system only takes sequential, rather than concurrent trades, we do not have to worry about calculation of open profits – each time a trade entry is made the account is 100% in cash. No account for commission or slippage is made in the profit or loss calculations.

System Value	Maximum Points	Minimum Points	Win%	Average Winner	Average Loser	Points Profit
2.96	411.29	-104.51	62%	67.24	-98.61	89.71

This is a superior position-sizing algorithm compared to the fixed dollar system. The maximum drawdown in points is lower and the end profit is higher. This strategy adapts to changes in account value and sizes smaller when losing and bigger when winning – this has the overall effect of giving a better return:risk ratio for the system as a whole (measured by system value).

⚖ System 10 – Averaging Down

System 10 uses the same fixed percentage method as System 9, but adds to losing trades when they have reached a certain loss point. This version of the system only adds to trades once. It is feasible to add in multiple units rather than only one and to have addition points that are based on profit per unit risk (R) or volatility rather than a fixed value. This level of testing is beyond the scope of this book, but the code at the end of the book could easily be adapted to test the effects of those position-sizing strategies.

System Value	Maximum Points	Minimum Points	Win%	Average Winner	Average Loser	Points Profit
-2.30	620.15	-203.85	65%[5]	54.64	-110.36	-127.73

Here we can see the effect of adding to a losing position (only once). The system value has now turned negative (and remember this is for a positive-expectancy set of trades!). The minimum points value is the lowest of all the systems so far, the average losing trade is double the average winner, and the total net profit in points is now negative. Also, this performance degradation does not take into account increased slippage and commission due to splitting trades into 2 units: A good example of what not to do.

⚖ System 11 – Scaling In

System 11 uses the same fixed percentage method as Systems 9 and 10, but adds to winning trades once they have reached a certain profit point. This version of the system only adds to trades once. It is feasible to add in multiple units rather than only one and to have additional points that are based on profit per unit risk (R) or volatility rather than a fixed value. Again, this level of testing is beyond the scope of this book but the example code could be enhanced to see the effects.

System Value	Maximum Points	Minimum Points	Win%	Average Winner	Average Loser	Points Profit
5.185	699.22	-208.87	57%[6]	81.94	-90.89	312.65

This technique results in a healthy system value, a good ending points profit and average winner versus loser size that is acceptable. Overall the most reasonable position sizing technique tested.

---

[5] The win% in this case has gone up because some of the additional trades were winners
[6] The win% has gone down in this case because some of the additional trades were losers

ᵻ System Comparison Summary

System	Value	Max. Points	Min. Points	Win%	Avg. Win	Avg. Lose	Points Profit
6	7.97	303.05	-162.15	62%	38.67	47.80	140.74
7	20.49	448.22	-29.86	62%	61.83	54.11	448.22
8	0.97	277.73	-134.82	62%	46.85	-72.79	21.66
9	2.96	411.29	-104.51	62%	67.24	-98.61	89.71
10	-2.30	620.15	-203.85	65%	54.64	-110.36	-127.73
11	5.185	699.22	-208.87	57%	81.94	-90.89	312.65

As we can see from the System Value score for each system, apart from the Martingale strategy used in System 7 which has unlimited risk, the best overall performer is fixed percentage position-sizing with scaling into winning positions (**System 11**).

ᵻ System Equity Curves

The system equity curves shown on the following pages are all to the same scale so it is easy to see the differences in volatility for each position-sizing method.

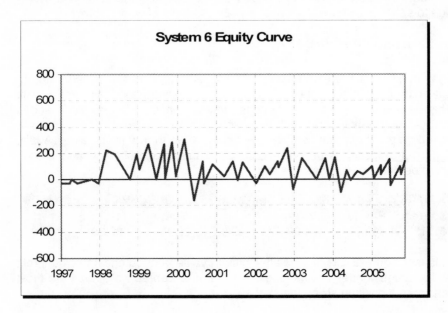

Figure 7: System 6 Equity Curve

100

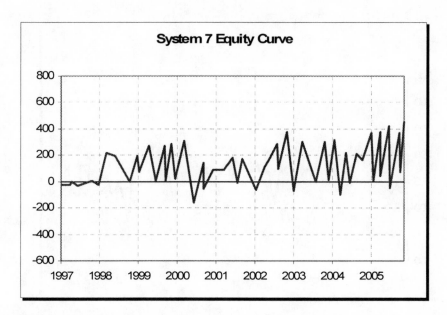

Figure 8: System 7 Equity Curve

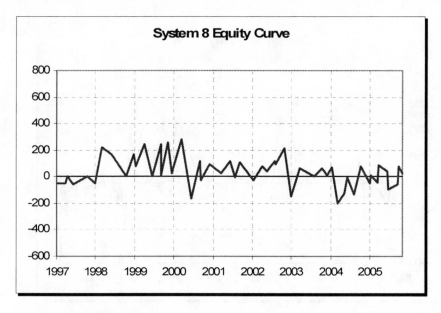

Figure 9: System 8 Equity Curve

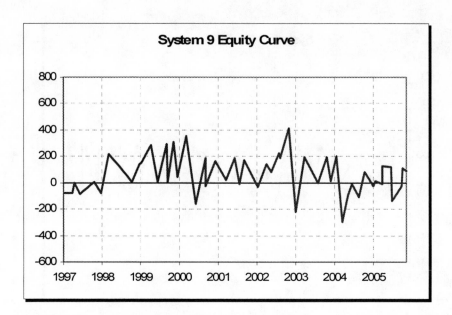

Figure 10: System 9 Equity Curve

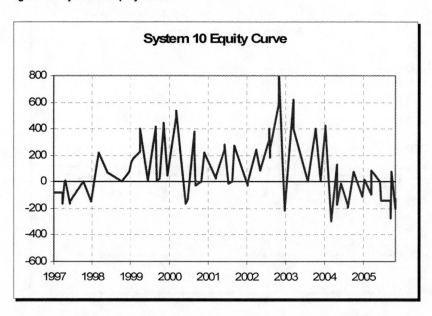

Figure 11: System 10 Equity Curve

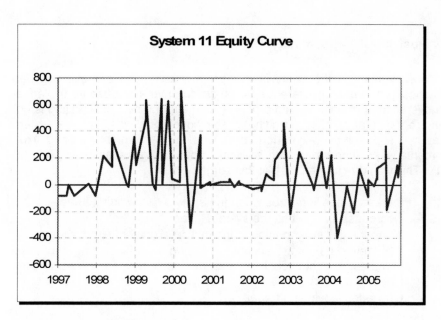

Figure 12: System 11 Equity Curve

♟ Position-Sizing Summary

Each system using the same instrument and entry and exit strategy was historically tested with different position-sizing criteria to observe the effect on overall performance (with the normal caveats that historical testing is not truly representative of real trading). The conclusion was that the system that had superior overall performance was the system that utilized fixed percentage position-sizing with scaling-in to winning trades only (**System 11**). This was due to the fact that this strategy:

- Increases position-sizes when the system has winning trades
- Decreases sizes when the system loses
- Manages risk in proportion to the capital allocated to the system
- Will never risk your account "blowing up" (assuming the fixed percentage is not too high and you don't have any losers much bigger than -1R)
- Only adds to winning trades

As you can see from the system results, position-sizing is what determines the volatility (or the smoothness) of the equity curve and the absolute performance of the system even when each one has exactly the same trades to work with. Position-sizing can be used to meet your objectives for reward and risk (assuming the system has a core positive expectancy). Each system exhibits different return and reward characteristics even though the instrument traded, testing period, and entry criteria are identical in each case.

Consequently, choosing the right position-sizing strategy for your requirements is a very important part of your system development since it determines whether the results you achieve from trading any particular system will meet your objectives.

How to match your position-sizing strategy to your objectives can be achieved once you can estimate the likely variability of the results you can expect from your system. Simulation is a useful technique for achieving this and is the topic of the next section.

♟ The Importance of Simulation

The single equity curve generated by most system testing environments (or your own real life trading) is "one-dimensional" in that it does not say much about the expected variability of the results. It is therefore difficult to effectively position-size a trading system to meet your objectives simply from a single (hypothetical or real) equity curve. You could use the amplitude of your equity curve (or wave) as an indication of variability but again, this is just a one-dimensional view based on a single sample.

One useful technique for assessing what "good and bad" could look like for your trading system or method, is to simulate the variability of your results to generate a series of "what if" situations (i.e. a set of equally likely equity curves). This gives you a much better indication of the possible range of results of your trading simply by showing what an equity curve would look like by randomly sampling the trades (or sequences of trades) in different orders.

In this section we look at simple but effective techniques for simulating the variability of your trading results in order to more effectively position-size a trading system to stay within your targets for reward and risk.

The main caveats of simulation are also discussed and these include:

- Future performance could be different than in the past
- Changes in implementation costs could affect actual results
- Implementation errors can be a significant factor
- Serial dependency changes can invalidate simulation results
- Concurrent trades are not considered
- Intra-trade performance is not considered (i.e. trades are considered "atomic" in that they can't be split)
- Position-sizing effects can alter the results

If done properly, simulation of the variability of results can be a great benefit in setting sensible position-sizing rules and also setting your expectation for "what good looks like" and knowing when a trading system or method is operating within or outside normal parameters. If you know what the likely range of results is for your system you can have rules in place that monitor, detect, and actually do something about situations where your trading is not acting "normally" before things go from bad to worse.

↓ When Expectancy Isn't Useful

First we must discuss the need for simulation and situations when simple expected value (or reward per unit risk) is not a useful measure to effectively position-size a trading system.

Imagine a simple coin-tossing game where you won 2 units for a head, 4 units for 2 heads in a row, 8 units for 3 heads in a row, doubling the payout each time for each consecutive head.

For tails, you would lose 1 unit for 1 tail, 2 units for 2 tails in a row, 4 units for 3 tails in a row etc.

One "turn" of the game would be to toss the coin until you got a tail (i.e. a losing turn). The expectancy for this game is theoretically infinite since there is no theoretical limit to the number of heads one can get in a row for a turn. The theoretical maximum loss is also infinite. How much would you pay to play each turn of this game?

Let's say you do one trial run of 10 tosses and get the following results where H=heads, and T=tails:

HTHHTTHHHT

This would result in the following payouts:

H	= +2 units
T	= -1 unit
HH	= +4 units
TT	= -2 units
HHH	= +8 units
T	= -1 unit

Thus the total winnings were 10 units. If you divide this by 6 turns you made 1.667 units per trial so you could assume that is a good price to pay for one "turn". However if we re-order the sample so all the tails come first we get the following results:

TTTTHHHHHH

Which would give us -8 + 64 = +56 units with an average win per turn of 56/2 = 28. This is a completely different result for the first test with the same number of heads and tails just in a different order.

ꞏ Payouts and Probabilities

If we say the game can only be played in a series of 10 tosses then the expectancy is no longer infinite – there are the following combinations of turns with the following probabilities:

Possible Turn	Payout	Probability	Expectancy (Payout * Probability)
HHHHHHHHHH	1024	0.000977	1.0
HHHHHHHHH	512	0.00195	1.0
HHHHHHHH	256	0.00391	1.0
HHHHHHH	128	0.00781	1.0
HHHHHH	64	0.01563	1.0
HHHHH	32	0.03125	1.0
HHHH	16	0.0625	1.0
HHH	8	0.125	1.0
HH	4	0.25	1.0
H	2	0.5	1.0
T	-1	0.5	-0.5
TT	-2	0.25	-0.5
TTT	-4	0.125	-0.5
TTTT	-8	0.0625	-0.5
TTTTT	-16	0.03125	-0.5
TTTTTT	-32	0.01563	-0.5
TTTTTTT	-64	0.00781	-0.5
TTTTTTTT	-128	0.00391	-0.5
TTTTTTTTT	-256	0.00195	-0.5
TTTTTTTTTT	-512	0.000977	-0.5

The average expected payout is 0.25 units per turn for this game.

The maximum win (for 10 heads in a row) is 1024 and the maximum loss (for 10 tails in a row) is -512. This does not really give us a useful value to "price" a turn. The probability of ten heads in a row is 0.5 to the power 10 which is 0.000977 which gives us an expected value of 1.0 for this combination. In fact all the winning combinations have an expected value (payout multiplied by probability) of 1.0 compared to the losing ones of -0.5.

The loss for 10 tails in a row is -512 (with the same probability of 0.000977) so the expected loss for this combination is -0.5 units. The average expected payout overall for all cases (winners and losers) is 0.25 units. Is that a better estimate for the value of a turn? It sounds quite low to me. Does this give a useful answer for how much to pay per turn? Not really.

1   Using Simulation

What we really want to know is that practically if we play this game what kind of results are we likely to get. An example simulation of 10,000 trials of the game (up to 10 tosses for each trial) yields the following frequency distribution:

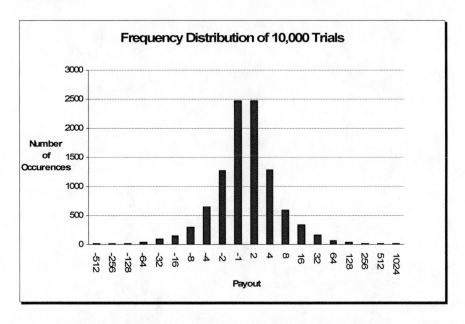

The chart above shows the number of occurrences (out of the total of 10,000) of each possible turn payout (-512 to +1024).

In this particular example the average value of one turn of the game is about 2.75 units (for this particular set of trials). Paying less than 2.75 units per turn to play the game would be a good deal. If you had criteria for maximum and minimum drawdown then you could use the simulation results to "position size" each bet based on winning (or losing) multiples of your unit bet. If we run the simulation many times we get a range of results that indicate that each turn is worth between about 2.5 and 3.5 units so this gives us a reasonable range for the expected payout in practical terms.

These numbers are higher than the mathematical probability calculation because of the relatively tiny probability of the "extremes" of heads and tails in a row, and the much more common distribution of turns that are only 2, 3, or 4 heads or tails in a row. As you can see from the distribution most of the turns are +2 or -2 units (from 1 or 2 heads or tails in a row respectively).

The simulation gives us a better "real life" answer than mathematical probability calculations. With real trading the actual distribution of winning and losing trades is not known in advance (and is also variable) so simulation is significantly more useful than simple probability calculations in demonstrating what expected results will look like with different trade ordering.

Generally a series of "equally likely" equity curves using a sample trade distribution gives us a much more useful picture with which to position-size our trading system. This topic is covered in the rest of this section.

⚖ Your Objectives

Before anything useful can be derived from a simulation of hypothetical or real trading results, we must already know what our expected risk and reward profile is. If you don't know how much you want to make (or how much you are prepared to risk to achieve the desired return), simulation of the variability of results is of little value.

At the very least you should know what your maximum tolerable loss of initial capital is. This can then be used to position-size against some "worst-case" estimate derived from your simulation results. In the game situation previously described the absolute "worse-case" loss was -512 units. Using this as our practical limit to what we should expect to lose would result in position-sizing that was much too small to even justify playing the game. A much more useful method would be to simulate the game to see what a worse-case practical amount to lose over, say, 100 turns was, and then use that to position-size accordingly.

Although it is theoretically possible for the S&P 500 to go to zero by the end of the week, if we used that as an estimate for a practical "worse case" scenario it would mean we would be sizing our positions so small as to make no difference what happened (good or bad). Trading is a practical risk-taking endeavor and therefore any representation of risk must be practical and reasonable.

⚖ Serial Dependency

Serial dependency is the tendency for some trading system to generate "clusters" of trades (either winners or losers) condensed into certain time periods. If this is the case then simulating the variability of results by randomizing the trade order will not be representative of the real trading system (since the clustering will be lost in single-trade randomization).

Before we can simply simulate our trading system by "scrambling" sets of trades and seeing what the possible outcomes are, we must determine that there is no serial dependency between trades. If, for example, winners tend to follow winners, or losers follow losers, then this relationship would be lost by scrambling our trade order. This could make our simulation an ineffective representation of what could really happen.

The simplest way to test for serial dependency between trades is to calculate the number of different combinations of 2 trades:

Win-Win
Win-Loss
Loss-Win
Loss-Loss

The occurrence of these pairs should then be compared to the probability of the pair existing within the whole sample based on the win%. For example, if you have 55% winners then the probability of each of the pair types is shown below:

Trade Pair	Probability	Expected Approximate Occurrence Percentage
Win-Win	0.55*0.55 = 0.3025	30%
Win-Loss	0.55*0.45 = 0.2475	25%
Loss-Win	0.45*0.55 = 0.2475	25%
Loss-Loss	0.45*0.45 = 0.2025	20%

If the actual percentage of the pairs within the whole sample is significantly different from their probability then there may be a serial dependency in your sample. Any serial dependency needs to be preserved when the simulation is conducted in order that the results are truly representative. For example, if the number of "Loss-Loss" pairs in our sample was considerably different than about 20% then we may have a serial dependency between losing trades; i.e. they tend to come all together. This kind of test can also be conducted on combinations of 3 or more trades in a similar manner.

The easiest method of preserving serial dependency during simulation is to simulate sequences of trades rather than single trades. The number of trades to "lump" together to preserve the dependency can be calculated relatively easily. Increase the set of trades you do the above test with until you get no difference in the expect percentage of that trade combination versus the actual percentage expected; that will determine your "chunk" size. Instead of simulating random combinations of one trade, simulate random combinations of your "chunk size" number of trades. The simulation examples in the rest of this section have no serial dependency so the simulation used simply randomizes the individual trades rather than using "chunks" of trades.

Choosing the best "chunk" size for your particular trading system or method can be trial-and-error to see how the simulation changes with the different number of trades.

⚥ Example Simulation

Sample R multiples for PMKing Trading's ModeX intra-day futures trading system, applied to the S&P500 e-mini (ES) futures contract between 9/28/04 and 8/16/6 were used. R is a measure of profit (or loss) per unit risk as determined by the initial stop. In this case the system was tested assuming no position-sizing algorithm, i.e. using 1 contract per trade.

Each R value was calculated by using the following formula:

End Profit or Loss / Absolute (Entry Price – Initial Stop Price)

The generated R-values are shown below:

1.13	0.26	3.60	-0.53	3.80	0.09	-0.50	-0.35	-0.29
-0.93	-0.36	-0.25	-0.52	0.96	0.00	0.08	0.31	-0.35
-0.77	-0.40	0.00	-0.43	-0.20	-0.33	-0.06	6.00	0.31
1.29	-0.73	-0.59	0.00	-0.58	-0.38	-0.57	-1.07	6.00
1.25	-0.36	-0.11	0.70	-0.36	3.09	-1.22	-0.25	-1.07
2.35	-0.53	2.31	-0.48	-0.33	1.75	-1.11	-0.05	-0.25
-0.79	1.29	-0.31	-0.15	-0.33	-0.35	-0.18	-0.56	-0.05
2.87	2.92	-0.75	0.76	-0.80	-0.89	-0.62	-0.15	-0.56
0.00	1.55	-0.50	-0.45	0.80	-0.79	0.50	-0.15	-0.15
-0.30	-0.67	3.13	-0.57	-0.18	-0.12	-0.35	0.00	-0.15
-0.13	0.75	-0.13	-0.17	1.68	-0.44	-0.20	2.14	0.00
-0.30	-0.33	1.08	0.33	-0.39	1.22	3.67	2.70	2.14
2.33	0.25	0.13	1.19	-0.73	-0.25	-0.38	0.00	2.70
-0.15	-0.07	0.00	1.75	-0.50	0.72	-0.57	0.00	0.00
-0.25	-0.05	-0.56	-0.15	-0.15	0.00	2.14	2.70	-0.29
0.00	-0.29	-0.35	-1.07	1.00	0.31	-0.35		

The average R multiple (or E) is 0.314 for this sample. Simulation of a negative expectancy sample is not generally useful since any positive equity curves generated are simply due to chance and do not mean the system has any real value.

Percentage changes in equity on a per-period basis can also be used for simulation purposes. I prefer to use R so that we can subsequently set R to a particular percent of account value according to our requirements for maximum risk and reward thresholds.

₤ Serial Dependency Test

The serial dependency test shows the following results:

Actual Win%   38%
Actual Loss% 62%

Expected Frequency of Win-Win = 0.38*0.38 = 15%
Expected Frequency of Loss-Loss = 0.62*0.62 = 38%

Actual Frequency of Win-Win = 14%
Actual Frequency of Loss-Loss = 38%

Since the actual occurrence of pairs of winning and losing trades is very close to the expected occurrence if the distribution was random, then there are no serial dependence issues with our set of R-multiples in this particular case.

The fact that there is no serial dependency between trades means we can proceed with a simple simulation that randomizes the order of single trades; rather than worrying about simulating sequences or chunks of trades to attempt to preserve the serial dependency in the sample.

₤ The Simulation

The simulation results shown below were created in a spreadsheet program by sampling random sets of 100 trades from the R-multiple distribution 100 times. The number of simulations or trades sampled can be increased, but in my experience 100 trades sampled 100 times is sufficient to create representative results. The resulting equity curves (in units of cumulative R) were then analyzed. If there is a serial dependency in your R multiple distribution then it is recommended that you sample sets of more than 1 trade (e.g. groups of 2, 3, or more) to preserve the serial dependency during your simulation.

± Equity Curves (in R)

The simulated equity curves for the R-multiple distribution are shown below. The "Best 100 Actual Trades" represents the equity curve that made the most (in R) from 100 sequential trades selected from the actual R-multiple sample without changing the ordering. The "Worst 100 Actual Trades" represents the equity curve that made the least (in R) from 100 trades selected from the actual R-multiple sample without changing the ordering.

The thin grey lines represents the 100 "equally likely" equity curves that could have resulted from the trades generated by randomly sampling from the given set of R multiples.

Legend

Best 100 Actual Trades
Worst 100 Actual Trades

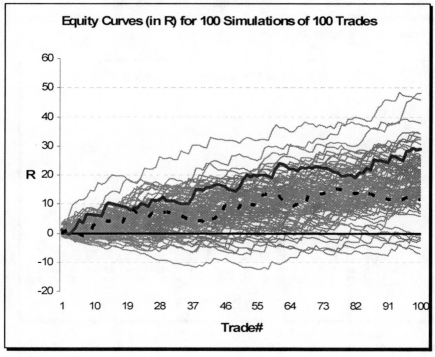

Figure 13: 100 Simulated Equity Curves

As we can see from the sample we should expect to make a maximum of about 45R in 100 trades and could actually lose -10R in 100 trades as a worse-case scenario with this particular sample of trades.

This gives us a much more detailed picture than 100 trades at 0.314R per trade which equals 3.41R profit based on the expectancy of the whole sample.

↧ Frequency Distribution

The frequency distribution (**Figure 14** below) shows the percentage of the simulated trades that were for a particular R profit (positive values) or R loss (negative values). As we can see this system generates a lot of small losers; nearly one third are -0.3R losses. There were no losers greater than -1R which indicates no implementation errors or significant slippage.

This happens to be a pure intra-day system that does not take overnight positions so there would have to be exceptional circumstances to get much larger than -1R losers. This also effectively limits the maximum winning trade size due to trade durations, so there are relatively few large (i.e. greater than 2R) winners.

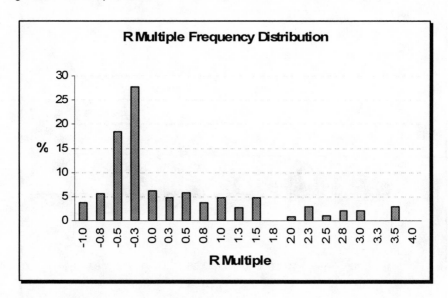

Figure 14: Simulation Frequency Distribution

The frequency distribution tells us whether our winning trades are a few big winners, a lot of small winners, or some combination of the two. In this case we see we are cutting losses short by having lots of small losers, and letting profits run, to some extent, because we see a reasonable distribution of winners up to 1.5R.

This distribution is an important indicator of where the reward and risk is coming from in your trading system. It also indicates whether there are any anomalous big winners, or greater than 1R losers.

⅄ Summary Data

The summary statistics shown below are taken from the same simulation. Key data attributes will now be discussed.

Simulation Summary Statistics

Highest Ending R	42.17	Start Date	08/05/04	
Lowest Ending R	-9.92	End Date	08/18/06	
Highest Ever R	45.23	Days in Test	743	
Lowest Ever R	-9.92			
%Positive Ending R	98%			
%Negative Ending R	2%	Trades per Day	0.19	
Highest/Lowest Ratio	4.56	Days per Trade	5.23	
Standard Deviation	9.23	# of Trades	142	
Best R Per Year	29.42	Simulation#	100	of 100
Worst R Per Year	-6.92	Trade#	100	of 100
%Winners	35%			
%Losers	65%			
		Max. Wining Streak	8	(+9.05R)
Average Winner	1.38R	Max. Losing Streak	18	(-7.47R)
Average Loser	-0.44R	Largest Single Win	+3.80R	
Breakeven Win%	24%	Largest Single Loss	-1.22R	

Highest Ending R

This is the highest ending equity value after 100 trades. It represents the "best case" scenario for this R-multiple distribution. At 42.17R this represents a win of 0.42R (on average) per trade and is higher than the expected profit of 31.4R based on the sample.

Lowest Ending R

This is the lowest ending equity value after 100 trades. It represents the "worst case" scenario for this R-multiple distribution. At -9.92R this represents a loss of -0.09R (on average) per trade.

Highest Ever R

45.23R is the highest point on any simulated equity curve at any time during the simulation.

Lowest Ever R

A -9.92R loss is the lowest point on any simulated equity curve at any time during the simulation.

Best R Per Year

This is the "best case" R per year made based upon the average trade duration and frequency of trades during the simulation. At 29.42R this tells us what a "best case" scenario for R per year is with this distribution assuming future trade frequency and duration remain constant.

Worst R Per Year

This is the "worst case" R per year loss based upon the average trade duration and frequency during the simulation. At -9.92R this tells us what a "worst case" scenario for R per year is with this distribution.

Breakeven Win%

This is the percentage of winning trades we need to break even given the average size of winners versus losers. At 24% this means we could only have 24% winners and still not lose any money. If this value is greater than 50% it would indicate that this system would likely not be profitable long-term; i.e. is based on a short-term anomaly that gives us a temporarily high win percentage.

Max Consecutive Wins

This represents the maximum number of winning trades, in a row, throughout the whole simulation and the number of R this winning streak represented. 8 winners in a row making 9.05R is a reasonable number given the win% of 35%.

Max Losing Streak

This represents the maximum number of losing trades, in a row, throughout the whole simulation and the number of R this losing streak represented. 18 losers in a row losing -7.47R is a reasonable number given the loss% of 65%.

⅄ Interpreting the Results

In order to effectively interpret your simulation results, you need to match the simulation data to your objectives for risk and reward, and then decide how to position-size your system. This allows you to set the value of R, relative to your account size, to a suitable value that is within your requirements.

For example, let's say you wanted to make 20% per year without losing more than 20% of your account value (again in a yearly period).

We can see from the simulation that a -9.92R per year loss is possible from this distribution, so if R was set at 2% of account value per trade, you would still be within your maximum loss percentage of 20%. With R=2%, also your best case scenario on a yearly basis would be (29.42R*2%)=58.8% which is way above your desired return.

A more conservative approach would be to set R=1% of account value. This would allow for an even worse losing streak case, and also still have a good probability of hitting your reward target.

Obviously the best and worst cases of performance also give us good thresholds for what normal operating performance is for this system and could act as a "red flag" if they are exceeded (both on the profit and the loss side). This can help to answer the common question of "How do I know when my system is broken?"

⊥ Simulation Caveats

Although the information provided by the simple simulation previously described can be very useful in position-sizing a trading system, there can be drawbacks to this method and some of the main caveats of this type of simulation include:

- Future performance could be different than in the past
- Changes in implementation costs could affect actual results
- Implementation errors can be a significant factor
- Serial dependency changes can invalidate simulation results
- Concurrent trades are not considered
- Intra-trade performance is not considered (i.e. trades are atomic)
- Position-sizing effects can alter results

Future Performance

As the regulatory disclaimer "Historical performance is no guarantee of future results" states, a simulation is using only historical data. Even if it is from real trades, there is no guarantee that the future distribution of winners and losers will be similar to the past. All we can hope for is that there is some resemblance between the future and the past. Re-running a simulation periodically with new data is also effective at adapting to changes in the way your trading system works. For this reason it should be a regular feature of your trade analysis not just a "one off" test performed when you initially develop and test a trading system.

Implementation Costs

If your historical data is hypothetical, rather than from real trades, and does not include an accurate representation of slippage, commissions, and other implementation costs then the simulation could overstate potential reward and understate potential draw-downs. Always assess the possible effect of implementation costs on your trading system. This is particularly important for high-frequency trading where implementation costs represent a much bigger proportion of possible reward than in long-term, low frequency trading.

Implementation Errors

No matter what your simulation shows, if you do not implement your system as designed (and simulated) due to implementation errors (for whatever reason), your simulation results will not be representative. Tracking implementation errors to see how they usually decrease trading profit and increase draw-downs is important in identifying deviations from expected performance. This can be recorded as any deviation from actual R value versus expected R value and is referred to as D (for deviation).

Serial Dependency

As previously discussed, if there is a serial dependency in your trade distribution and this is not taken into account in the simulation, the results will not be representative. Usually the dependency means that there is a tendency for winning and losing trades to "cluster" together. Therefore if this is not preserved in the simulation the results will understate possible draw-downs and also under-state maximum returns. Testing for serial dependency should also be performed periodically in case it has been introduced in a system where it previously did not exist.

Having rules that automatically include a serial dependency in your trading systems (e.g. if a previous trade was a winner then .... do something different) should generally be avoided for this reason.

Concurrent Trades

Everything in the simulation techniques discussed so far assumed trades are sequential. Obviously this is not generally the case in real life where a system can take multiple concurrent trades. This means that the simulation results may understate both profits and drawdown on a per-time-period basis. This is because it would be possible to have multiple concurrent losers, whereas the simulation technique treats each trade as sequential, i.e. one at a time.

Intra-Trade Information

Since the R multiples for your trades are atomic, i.e. the R multiple is only known when the trade is closed, no information is contained in the simulation about what happened intra-trade. If you are seriously concerned about intra-trade performance then a simulation of account value percentage changes, on whatever time period you like, should be done in addition to the R-multiple one. Instead of simulating R-multiples, one could simulate percentage changes in account value on a daily, weekly, or monthly basis instead. Testing for serial dependency should still be done if you use account value percentage changes. In this case a "chunk" of percentage changes, rather than just one at a time, should be simulated to ensure any serial dependency is preserved.

Position-sizing Effects

Since the R multiples used for the simulation did not include any position-sizing, when this is introduced into your real trading it could effect the overall distribution of the trading, especially if your position sizing is proportional to some measure of account value. The effects of position-sizing algorithms on trading system performance are discussed in detail in the section starting on page 88.

⅄ Simulation Summary

Simulation of the variability of results for a series of real or hypothetical trades gives us a lot of useful information about what to expect from a trading system and allows us to make an informed decision about how to position-size to meet our objectives.

Simulation is an analysis that should be performed periodically every time we have a new set of statistically significant data, e.g. every 30 trades. Having a complete simulation of our trades can give us good boundaries for what "good" and "bad" should look like for our trading. It also allows us to have rules to suspend trading when a system is operating outside normal parameters.

Although there are several caveats to using and interpreting simulation results I believe it is a valuable and useful technique. Simulation should be incorporated into every trader's toolkit of useful trading system development and testing methods.

♟ The Remainder of the System Development Process

Once you have a tested, simulated system with appropriate position-sizing defined it is time to actually see whether the system can be implemented for real. This involves the last stages of system development, testing, and implementation as shown previously in **Figure 3** on page 63.

- Testing in real-time on paper
- Small money testing
- Optimization
- Implementation
- Capital Allocation

These steps will now be discussed.

♟ Real-time Paper Testing

Assuming the historical testing of the system yields positive results it is worthwhile testing the system on paper in real-time. This proves to us that we have not back-fitted the system to the data and demonstrates that the entry signals are generated at the desired frequency.

Again, at least 30 trades should be tested in real-time without changing any aspect of the system. If the system is still exhibiting positive expectancy similar to the historical testing it is time to trade it for real.

♟ Small Real Money Testing

The real-money testing is designed to do one thing, and that is make sure the system can actually be implemented as you have designed it. Minimal position sizing should be used – e.g. one contract, one share, one option contract. Again, 30 trades should be completed and the expectancy measured. This test will be representative of commissions and spread, but will underestimate the effects of slippage due to the small size.

1 Optimization

At this point we have a working system that will be put into production trading and it is time to decide whether to implement the system as tested so far. Alternatively we need to decide whether to set the best possible values for the main variables and go through the whole process of historical, paper trading, and small real money testing again.

If you do want to optimize your system, I would recommend finding the lowest and highest value for each variable that produces a positive expectancy system and then choosing the median value. This means you are not optimizing for maximum expectancy, but for the value that has the maximum number of positive expectancy instances of the system on either side of it.

Many trading-related books have whole chapters on optimization, and almost every piece of trading system testing software I know of has an optimization function. Unfortunately most of the time people, and the software they use, are optimizing for the wrong thing – and that is maximum net ending equity.

Optimization in this way has the big problem that you are fitting the system to historical data, and also optimizing for something that may not be your most important criteria. The way optimization is normally carried out is like attempting to design a car with the following features all at the same time:

- Acceleration: 0-60 miles per hour in 5 seconds
- Capacity: Carry 7 people in comfort
- Economy: 50 miles to the gallon

Obviously with car design there are some features that will just have to be compromised on and to achieve them all would require more than one vehicle. It is much more useful to use the following guidelines when considering system optimization.

- Optimize market selection and instrument filter to find the most liquid instruments.

- Optimize setup to find places where moves are likely to occur. Note not in any particular direction though – setup should not be generally considered to be predictive of the future.

- Optimize entry to give you the required average number of trades per period.

- Optimize exits to yield the desired ratio of average winner to average loser (which has nothing to do with win%).

- Optimize position-sizing to keep performance within your risk and reward requirements.

That's it – no curve-fitting, pattern matching, or beautiful historical equity curves that never continue into the future.

♨ System Implementation

Once you have tested your system with small size real-money, it is time to give it a full allocation of capital and incorporate it with your other trading systems. This is covered in detail in the section called **Capital Allocation Overview** starting on page 132.

In order to implement your system effectively you need a good handle on your trading environment and the broker(s) you will use for your trading account(s). In this section we discuss everything that is required to ensure you can always manage your positions whatever happens. **Figure 15** shows all the main components of a trading environment, and therefore everything that you need to have an alternative for if something breaks or fails. These will now be discussed.

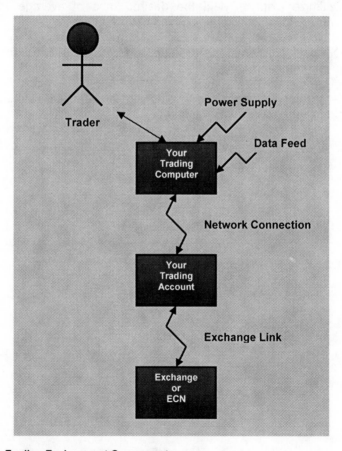

Figure 15: Trading Environment Components

⚖ Trading Technology

It has happened to all of us at some time. Just as we are about to enter or exit a position, something happens that prevents us from trading. It may be a computer crash, a power outage, or an internet connection problem, but whatever it is, did you have a backup plan and a way to work around the problem quickly enough to stop you from losing too much money?

⚖ Trader

Sometimes it is easy to forget that you are part of your trading environment. Even if you have automated mechanical systems, you need to monitor what is going on in case of a problem or unforeseen circumstance. If you are incapacitated or unavailable, due to a family emergency for example, who will take over as the backup trader and exit your positions?

You should always have a backup plan that includes someone else who knows how to access your trading account and exit your positions in the event that you are unable to. This person needs to know your account numbers and passwords, needs to be able to find out what positions you currently have, and needs the knowledge to effectively exit them without further instructions from you.

You also need a way of telling your backup trader that they need to take action; either electronically by email or instant message, by phone, or in person (if they work in the same location). It is always best to have written instructions which specifically list what the backup trader should do if they are called upon, and these instructions should be kept up to date when accounts, passwords, or other changes occur.

⚖ Trading Computer

If you are a completely paper-based trader and phone your orders to your broker, then this section of the book will be irrelevant to you, so skip to the next section which deals with your trading account.

Your trading computer is your connection to your trading account and there are many things that can go wrong to prevent you from being able to enter or exit positions when necessary. The computer itself can crash or break, the power supply could go out, your data feeds could stop working, your internet connection could go down, and your trading software could stop working.

Each of these needs an alternative. You need another computer setup that is equivalent to your main trading computer. You need a separate backup of all critical files so you can restore them to the alternate computer in case of a major crash. These files need to be offsite (in case of an office disaster), and readily accessible. One of the online backup services is a good choice since you can easily get your files back with just an internet connection and a backup computer.

Because your internet connection is so critical to most trading environments today, you need 2 types (e.g. a cable connection and a dialup one) in case one stops working. You also need an uninterruptible power supply so your modem and PC continues to work during a power outage, and you need 2 data feeds for each kind of price data your trading systems rely on in case one stops working temporarily.

ι Your Trading Account

The account at your prime broker's is the place where your trading capital lives. What will you do if your broker's servers go down and you cannot place any orders or access your account? In this case it is essential that you have a backup trading account at another broker that is funded with sufficient capital to reverse or hedge some positions. This means you can still manage positions in the event you cannot access your main brokerage account and you need to take action.

One way to do this is to split your trading capital in two, keep half with each broker, and then trade different systems in each account. In this way you should always be able to reverse a position in the event that one of your brokers has a problem.

ι Exchange or ECN

Each broker has links to the exchanges or Electronic Communications Networks (ECNs). Sometimes an exchange or ECN has a problem and cannot execute orders. In this case it is very important for you to know about an alternative trading venue or order execution destination for each of your positions so you can exit them even if the primary exchange on which they trade goes down. If you are trading instruments that only trade on one exchange then this is not possible, but most of the time you will be able to work out an alternative (but not necessarily perfect) instrument to trade on a trading venue that is still functioning.

For example, if you are trading the e-mini S&P 500 Futures contract on GLOBEX and the exchange has a technical problem you could trade an equivalent amount of SPY (S&P 500 SPYDRS) to hedge your futures position until GLOBEX comes back online. It is important that you understand what your alternative execution venues are, and what constitutes an 'equivalent position' before you place your trades, so you do not have to scramble to work it out when the primary exchange has a problem.

♪ Trading Technology Summary

Since trading involves computers, networks, and people, there will always be technical problems and failures. If you put a plan in place to have an alternative for each and every one of the components of your trading environment listed here, you will be much less likely to suffer a large loss due to your inability to exit a position when one of these problems (inevitably) occurs.

♪ Broker Selection

Choosing the correct broker to use to implement your trading system is an important consideration that should not just be made as a default by sticking with the broker you have always used for your trading or investing. Each brokerage has good and bad features specific to them, and not all will be equally suitable to each trading system you develop. The following section deals with some of the criteria that can be used to select a suitable broker for a particular trading system.

Instruments Traded

The most important aspect of the brokerage that is relevant to a particular system is whether the broker has good access (or any access) to trade the particular instrument the system was designed for. This depends on what exchange linkages the broker has, and whether they have access to all the possible trading venues for a particular instrument type. If they have multiple venues for one instrument then how do they allow you to route your order to the best available price, or via a preferred route? This "smart routing" technology (or lack of it) will affect the fills you get, the execution speed, and ultimately the slippage you encounter when you trade.

Exchange Linkages

Obviously in order to execute orders for your chosen instrument your broker needs to have access to the exchange upon which the instrument trades. It is essential in today's high-speed, high-technology markets that the broker has an electronic exchange linkage. You do not want your broker to be phoning in orders – ideally the whole route from your PC to the exchange will be electronic so that you can get filled at a price that is as close to the quoted price as possible when you entered the order.

Software/Order Management

The software that your broker provides to manage your account and especially to enter and execute orders is an important piece of your trading toolkit. If you are trading long-term with overnight positions with an average trade duration of weeks or months, then your needs are not so time critical and regular internet-based browser access to your account is acceptable. If you are trading intra-day with trade durations of a few minutes then it is essential that your broker's technology solution is fully-automated and fast enough to process orders almost instantly.

Margin

Although some margin rules are set by exchanges and regulatory bodies, brokers do have discretion about how they handle some margin decision. For example, some brokers will issue margin calls and ask for more cash before closing positions, whereas others will simply start closing positions to realize enough cash to cover margin requirements. Brokers also differ on how they pay interest, if at all, due to short-sale cash balances. Check your broker's margin rules to avoid an unexpected and costly mistake in the future. It's too late to complain about an automated exit of positions you wanted to stay in because of a margin problem with your account after it actually happens.

Fees and Commissions

How much brokers charge in commission varies significantly for basically the same commodity: order execution. Commissions can become a very significant part of the costs of running your trading business - especially for high-frequency trading. There is no point paying more than 1 cent per share for US equity trades, for example, if the execution quality of the major brokerage houses is all pretty much equivalent. Brokers can also charge other types of trade and account level fees, inactivity fees, low balance fees, etc. Choosing one that has low fees with your required level of exchange access and services can make a significant difference to your bottom line at the end of the year.

For some instrument types, commissions are not explicitly stated but are "hidden" in the quoted spread (for example, in foreign exchange trading). Obviously the wider the spread (the difference in the current selling and buying prices) the more you are actually paying each time you enter and exit a position. Check that the spreads that the broker is offering are competitive.

Cost of Carry Charges

For some instrument types there is an explicit charge (or credit) for holding a position. For example, for foreign exchange transactions the holder pays interest on the short side of the position and earns interest on the long side. The difference in the two interest rates is called the cost of carry - although it can sometimes be positive. Contract for Differences (CFDs[7]) also often have carry charges that are paid on long trades, and received on short ones. Ensure your broker's carry charges are reasonable, and also find out how often they change and publish the cost information. This can sometimes make the difference between a winning and losing trade if you hold long-term positions.

Capital Reserves

How much cash your broker has in its reserves is important. You don't want to find out your account has been wiped out by your broker going bankrupt. Although there are regulations that ensure segregation of customer funds from brokerage assets, it's not going to be much use to you that you will *eventually* get your money back and be able to resume trading if your broker goes bankrupt. Choosing a broker that has large cash reserves, a large number of active clients and a good balance sheet is an important consideration. Most brokers have to publish financial information on a yearly basis so that customers can make an informed decision.

Customer Service

One aspect of using a brokerage that is difficult to assess before using their service is their customer service. How reliable is it? How well do they respond when you have inevitable problems. I recommend monitoring how often you have "outages" in service and how quickly a brokerage responds to a query to assess their performance. Remember that no brokerage offers 100% uptime and response guarantees for the quality of their customer service. Normally this is a question of whether the brokerage is acceptable overall. If you stopped using a broker because of periodic outages, or the inability to get through to a real person on the phone, you wouldn't have any left to choose from after a couple of years.

---

[7] These are not legal trading instruments in the US

Online Features

How much online access you need is dependant on your own requirements and trading systems. Personally, I want to be able to do everything the brokerage offers online (including cash withdrawals, account management, and chatting to customer service representatives). In this way I only have to worry about the technology not working rather than the phone, the person at the other end, and myself all having to "be on the same page". Alternatively, you may like the reassurance of having a "real" person to talk to when you have problems. Some "full service" brokers offer this but usually charge hefty fees for this kind of personal "hand holding".

Types of Stops

Not all brokers offer all kind of orders, stops, and trade management features. For example some brokers don't even offer trailing stops. Sometimes the maintenance of them in their trading software is somewhat unreliable. Check whether the specific order types and features your trading system requires are implemented by reading the user guide for the trading software provided by your broker. Yes, actually read the manual! Most brokers now offer demonstration software complete with "pretend cash" accounts so you can fully test whether they meet your requirements before committing to opening an account. If you struggle with the testing environment then there is no hope for live trading with real money under pressure.

Account Types

Not all brokers offer all the different account types (e.g. Independent Retirement Accounts, Margin Accounts etc.) Check that the broker offers the type of account you need, and what restrictions there may be, if any, regarding cash balances, fees, exchanges and instruments traded in each account type, and margin rules.

⚐ Broker Selection Summary

As you can see there are a lot of considerations when choosing a broker and your backup broker in case your primary account is not accessible. It should also be an ongoing process, not a "one time" effort since broker policies, reliability, customer service quality, and capital reserves are all a moving target. Brokerage evaluation should be part of your annual review to make sure you are still happy with the service and there are no better alternatives available for you right now.

The last remaining steps required in your system implementation and management include:

- Capital Allocation
- Monitoring
- Retirement

These will now be discussed.

♟ Capital Allocation

Once you have multiple trading systems that each require capital (possibly in different accounts) then you have some more complicated decisions to make about how to apportion your available capital across each system.

The simplest method is to trade one system per account and allocate an equal amount of capital to each system. This solution can help minimize implementation errors caused by the complexity of managing multiple positions per system in one account. However, it is not usually practical to do this due to margin/leverage/capital usage considerations.

Some systems may have a higher minimum capital requirement than others. Some may have a much higher expectancy than others and there may be periods when certain systems are generating few signals. This means the capital allocated to them is not being fully utilized. If you trade one system per account it can lead to situations where you are not getting the best use of your available capital.

If you do decide to implement the simplest solution, then all you need are rules in place that say how often you will "rebalance" each account as necessary. In the case where some systems have been profitable and others have lost money, each account no longer has an equal capital allocation and capital may need to be shifted from the winning account to the losing one.

ⅰ Capital Allocation Overview

Effective allocation of trading capital across multiple trading systems is an important concept that allows us to maximize the return on each of our trading systems, and therefore our trading dollars, euros, yen etc.

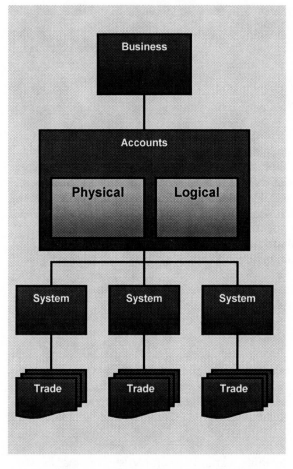

This section describes the four levels of capital allocation from the highest (business) to the lowest (trade) level. The levels of capital allocation discussed include:

- Business
- Accounts
- Systems
- Trades

Concepts that are explained, along with their practical application to trading, include:

- Position-sizing at the trade level
- Allocation methods for multiple trading systems
- Use of leverage and trading notional amounts
- Calculating system performance with a changing capital allocation

Figure 16: Capital Allocation Levels

Once you have read and understood the concepts in this section you will be able to easily define a capital allocation model at each level that suits your requirements and effectively uses an amount of leverage you are comfortable with (if any). You will also know how to allocate capital to each of your trading systems accordingly.

133

Once you have a suite of positive-expectancy trading systems, the way you allocate your available capital to them is one of the most important decisions you will make that determines the overall size and volatility of your trading returns.

ı The Four Levels of Capital Allocation

The four levels of capital allocation you need to consider from the largest to the smallest are:

- Business
- Accounts
- Systems
- Trades

Business level capital allocation determines what amount of capital (and therefore total risk) will be allocated for a trading business as a whole and this amount flows down to the other levels. Account level capital allocation determines how much business capital is actually available in each account including margin and leverage. The 'notional' amount you are trading may be higher than actual cash available due to margin facilities. System level capital allocation determines how much of your available capital is allocated to any individual trading system. At the trade level, capital allocation (also called position-sizing) determines how big to size an individual position.

A diagram of the levels of capital allocation is shown in **Figure 16** on page 133. Each of these levels will now be discussed.

ı Business Level

A trading business can be viewed as a collection of brokerage accounts that have trading capital in them. In the simplest form, the total business capital allocation is the sum of the cash in each of the brokerage accounts, but this does not necessarily equate to the total capital allocation that is appropriate for the business.

If we want to significantly reduce risk, either temporarily or permanently, we could have a business capital allocation that is only a percentage of the available capital, for example 50%. This would mean that the total capital available for trading would be half, and half would be kept in cash. Under these circumstances, if we have a rule that says we are only willing to take a total risk of 10% of allocated capital for the business as a whole, it would effectively cut our total risk in half.

Having this business-level rule that says that for all open positions, based on stop-loss points, total risk can never be greater than X% of the business capital allocation is an effective way to specify a worst-case loss point. It also puts a throttle on a system that is signaling too many trade entries in terms of total risk. This rule would also kick-in and temporarily reduce or suspend trading after a prolonged string of losses. This concept is commonly referred to as portfolio heat.

Alternatively, we could have a business-level capital allocation that is actually larger than real total cash. This is due to the effects of available margin, and other business and account-level regulations that allow us to hold bigger positions than the amount of cash we actually have. This is especially true for intra-day positions in the US. Generally, if you have a suite of dependable, positive expectancy trading systems, then you would want to maximize the business level capital allocation by trading as big as possible in each of the available accounts to maximize their individual margin usage. Note that this will maximize return, but will also maximize risk, and should only be done if you are very confident in your trading abilities and your trading systems. For novice traders, business-level capital allocation should be less than or equal to the total amount of cash in each of the accounts held by the business.

Although we can have a rule that determines a maximum amount of risk that we can take at the business level, the business-level capital allocation itself is mainly determined by the capital allocations of each of the accounts and this will be discussed next.

₤ Account Level

Accounts can be thought of as two main kinds: physical and logical. A physical account is an actual account at a brokerage firm that is funded with cash and has margin rules and can actually execute trades. A logical account is an account owned by the business (proprietary), or an external party (customer) and represents a notional amount of cash and positions. In the simplest case, the business will have one physical brokerage account, and simply trade that as one logic proprietary account, so there will be a 1:1 relationship between the 2 accounts.

In more complicated cases, a business may have more than 1 physical brokerage account. This may be used for trading different products, or as a backup if the main trading brokerage account is unavailable for some reason. The capital in these physical accounts may be allocated across multiple proprietary or customer accounts.

In a logical account, we can determine the exact capital allocation rules ourselves. We can determine the actual cash amount in the account and the notional amount in relation to actual cash depending on the type of trading systems we plan to trade in the account. For example, if we are only planning to trade an intra-day US equity trading system in a proprietary account, we could decide to set a notional amount in the account of 4 times the actual amount of cash in the account since current US pattern day trading margin rules dictate that we can have 4:1 leverage in a pattern day trader US dollar margin account.

If this is a proprietary account used for testing new trading systems we may decide to have a notional amount that is much smaller than actual cash in order to test a system without risking too much cash.

In cases where the notional amount traded is much higher than actual cash, there may be circumstances where new positions cannot be taken without reducing existing position sizes due to margin restrictions. In this case it is recommended that you downsize losing positions first, followed by positions that are in profit the least, or have been held for the longest time. The important thing is to have written rules that specify how you will handle these situations before they occur.

Since notional amounts that can be traded in a logical account are dependent on local margin regulations, it is impossible to give a fixed way of setting this amount. As a guide I can say that for logical accounts that trade intra-day systems, I use a notional amount that is a multiple of actual cash (to take intra-day margin into account). For longer-term systems I use a notional that is equal to cash, or smaller, depending on whether the trading environment is unsuitable for that particular trading system. Overall you want to set a notional amount that maximizes margin usage across all accounts to get maximum "bang for your buck".

This leads us on to system-level capital allocation, since any logical account capital allocation is always dependent on the types of trading system that will be traded in the account.

ⅼ System Level

At the simplest level, with only one trading system, it is relatively easy to allocate capital to a system. It is simply the sum of the notional capital allocations for all accounts that will trade the system. If multiple trading systems are being traded simultaneously, then we need more sophisticated methods for allocating capital to each one. There are various ways to do this and we will work from the least to most sophisticated approaches.

⚖ Fixed Equal Capital Allocation

A simple approach to system-level position sizing is to divide the total notional amount available by the number of trading systems and keep this as a fixed allocation throughout the year. This has the advantage that it is easy to do, and can easily be recalculated if capital is added to or withdrawn from the accounts. The disadvantage of this approach is that it does not reward winning systems either based on their historical performance relative to other systems, or on the amount they win during the year. Lastly, it does not reduce capital allocation to systems that go through a significant losing period, since they maintain the same allocation as a system that has been winning.

System Expectancy

In order to have a more sophisticated approach to capital allocation to each system we must have a way to 'score' the performance of each system relative to each other. System expectancy is a way of measuring the expected return per unit risked, and is calculated using the following formula:

Expectancy $E = \Sigma R$ / Number of Trades

Where R is the realized profit or loss on a trade divided by the initial risk being taken (based upon entry price, initial stop, and size).

⚖ Proportional Allocation Based on System Expectancy

Therefore, a more sophisticated way of allocating capital is to allocate to each system in proportion to the recent historical expectancy of the system. For example, if you had 3 systems with all-time expectancies of 0.25, 1.1, and 0.75 then they would receive the following percentages of available capital:

System	System Expectancy	Proportional Calculation	Percentage Allocation
1	0.25	0.25/(0.25+1.1+0.75)	12%
2	1.1	1.1/(0.25+1.1+0.75)	52%
3	0.75	0.75(0.25+1.1+0.75)	36%

The allocation would be calculated and allocated when the system started trading and could be reset each year. This method has the advantage that it rewards systems that have a higher expectancy with more cash to trade, but does not adjust capital allocation as systems make or lose money except on a yearly basis. Either recent (based on last X trades) or all-time expectancy could be used, and this could be recalculated periodically (e.g. weekly), after a certain number of trades, or even after each trade. Since expectancy is only recalculated based on closed trades, this allocation model will not effect open positions for a system.

If choosing to calculate expectancy based on recent trades it is recommended that a sample of at least 30, be used, and 100 would be better. This is to ensure that your sample expectancy is statistically significant and truly representative of the system's recent performance.

System Value

If we want to take into account not only the expectancy of a system, but also the volatility of the expectancy, and the number of trades the system makes, we can use a more sophisticated 'score' for the system called System Value. This is calculated using the following formula:

System Value V = (E $_{SYSTEM}$ / Standard Deviation of (R $_{SYSTEM}$)) * Number of Trades per Year

Where **E = Expectancy** which is **Average(R)** and **R** is the **Profit or Loss** divided by **Initial Risk** (as a positive number based on the difference between your entry price and your initial stop multiplied by your position size).

We can then use System Value as a more representative measure of system performance and allocate capital in proportion to that, rather than pure expectancy.

ᴪ Adjustable Proportional Allocation Based on System Value

In order to implement a 'survival of the fittest' type of capital allocation we can allocate proportionally based on System Value. We can also recalculate the System Value after every closed trade, and add all realized profits and losses to the original allocation to calculate a system's current capital allocation. This method can be used on an ongoing basis, or reset at the start of each trading year. Allocating capital in this way rewards systems that have high System Value, and that are currently making money, and takes capital away from systems that are not.

⅄ Adjustable Proportional Allocation Based on System Value within Market Type

One of the most sophisticated capital allocation models also uses System Value to proportionally allocate capital to systems, but also calculates the System Value for each of the nine types of market. Markets are classified based on trend and volatility and then the System Value is calculated for trades within each market type. Capital is then allocated in proportion to the System Value for the *current* market type. This process ensures that the systems get a capital allocation, in proportion to their value, that is specifically tailored to the prevailing market type. More detailed information about market classification is covered in the section called **Market Types**, on page 65.

⅄ Trade Level

Once we have a sophisticated capital allocation method for each of the trading systems we trade, the last level we need to consider is how much of the allocation we can apply to each individual trade a system signals. Position sizing for individual trades involves the following variables:

- Percentage of allocated capital to risk
- Entry price
- Initial stop loss
- Current capital allocation
- Current positions total risk percentage

Generally it is conservative to risk 1% of allocated capital per trade, but aggressive trading can risk up to 3%. Setting your percentage risk to meet your objectives was covered in the section called **The Importance of Simulation** starting on page 105. A good way to approach this is to start at 1% risk per position, and increase it in 1% increments as a system makes positive returns for the year. For example, you could have a percentage risk allocation model that has the following thresholds:

System Profit	Risk per Trade
0-10%	1%
10-20%	2%
>20	3%

If you are constantly changing the amount of capital allocated to a system due to additions and withdrawals of capital or adjustable capital allocation methods, then the average amount allocated to the system needs to be calculated. This allows us to calculate the percentage return for a system in a more representative way and I call this the Average Daily Allocation (ADA).

The Average Daily Allocation (ADA) is represented by the following formula:

ADA = Σ (Capital Allocated * Number of Days) / Total Days

And the system profit is defined as:

Total Profit / ADA

For example, if a system has $100,000 allocated for 10 days, and then $200,000 allocated for 20 days, and the total profit is $15,000 then the system profit is equal to:

$15,000/((100,000*10 + $200,000*20)/30)=$15,000/$166666=9%

Thus in our example the system has generated a 9% return and so should use a 1% of current allocation risk per trade since this is less than the 10% threshold we defined previously. Once we have determined the risk per trade (as a percentage of the current capital allocation) it is simple to size an individual position by using the formula:

Position Size = (%risk * current allocation)/(absolute(entry price – initial stop loss)

Obviously, unless you have a pre-defined initial stop loss, it is impossible to sensibly define your risk and therefore what size to trade. It is recommended that you always have an initial stop loss calculation as part of your trading system definition. This point should be far enough out of the daily noise of the market to indicate that your trade is not working. If you do not have the initial stop loss point, and therefore initial risk is not defined, it is not possible to calculate expectancy.

Most effective stop loss points are based on a multiple of recent volatility in the instrument being traded. The 2 main measures of volatility are trading range based (e.g. Average True Range), or Standard Deviation Based (e.g. Standard deviation of Close). It is usually best to multiply your volatility measure by a factor that is suitable for the length of time you intend to stay in the trade. For example, for a trade that lasts 1-5 days, 1-2.5 times the recent Average True Range over the last 5 days would be a good initial stop point. If your system is based on a breakout of a range, or crossing a moving average, then it may also be possible to use these points as an initial stop loss that indicates the trade is not working as planned. The section called **The Importance of Exits**, starting on page 72, covered exit strategies in detail.

Lastly, I should mention that it is sensible to have a maximum number of open positions, or a maximum total percentage risk parameter for any particular trading system. This parameter is designed to limit the maximum risk an individual system may take and works by either scaling down existing positions, or temporarily suspending new positions from being entered. This prevents us taking too much risk on one particular trading system (even if it is going through a winning streak) and prevents diversification being undermined.

⅄ Capital Allocation Summary

In this section we have discussed the four different levels of capital allocation and the way they need to be considered to manage risk when trading multiple systems. We have described methods for allocating capital from the trade level right up to the business level, and the ways in which they are related.

In all cases good capital allocation is designed to make the most effective use of available trading capital within the parameters you set for risk and reward.

1   Monitoring

Once your system is in "live" implementation with a defined capital allocation the only other tasks left to plan are:

- How you will minimize implementation errors

- How you will know if your system is operating properly

- What you will do if your system starts operating outside "normal" parameters

Reducing implementation errors is primarily about you having the discipline to accurately implement your system and this is covered in detail in **Part III** of this book.

The other part of accurate implementation is dependant on robust and reliable technology (hardware, software, and communications systems) and backups. This was discussed in the **Contingency Planning** section in **Part I** of this book.

Knowing when your system is operating properly is dependent on your simulation results and how you defined your position sizing rules based on those results. Repeating your simulation as your system generates new trades can help understand whether variability is increasing, staying the same, or decreasing. This was covered in the sections called **The Importance of Position Sizing,** starting on page 86, and **The Importance of Simulation,** starting on page 105.

Monitoring actual real-time results versus any historical back-testing results (that can be continued on a going-forward basis) is also a useful indicator. There may be reasons why the real-time results differ from those generated by your historical testing that need to be accounted for. For example, you may get much better results on the "cleaned" version of tick data used in historical testing compared to the real-time tick data used to actually trade your system. Sometimes these differences are enough to invalidate your system and that is why you should conduct small-size real-money testing before giving your system a full allocation of capital.

Checking the expectancy of your system on an ongoing basis (within each of the different market types previously discussed) is important to see if it is operating as your historical and small-size testing indicated.

If your results are "outside of normal parameters" based on your simulation expectations, and can't be accounted for by implementation errors that have subsequently been fixed, then you should revert to paper-trading until performance changes or you discover what the problem is. If you feel the urge to "twiddle" with your system based on isolated examples of losing trades, you should treat it as a completely new system development and go through the whole process of testing again from start to finish. I know nobody is going to do this but that's my advice anyway.

"Tweaking" your system based on the first few, losing, real-money, trades is a recipe for disaster. Why should you invalidate all of your previous design and testing based on a couple of losers? As long as they were less than 1R losers they are a perfectly normal part of trading and completely expected as part of your trading system design.

All systems go through losing periods, and as long as the size is proportional to your pre-defined risk tolerance then your system is not broken, it's just not making money right now.

⅃ Implementation Errors

Implementation errors are situations where the actual trade, or trades, you place were not identical to the ones signaled by your system. Anything that prevents you from implementing the trade exactly as defined by your system or method is an implementation error. Causes of implementation errors usually fall into one of the following categories:

- Technical Problems
- Psychological Problems

Technical problems preventing accurate implementation are an indication of an incomplete contingency plan where the backup for your primary way of implementing your trading system did not function correctly.

Psychological errors are anything where you were the cause of the deviation in some way. These will be covered in much more detail in **Part III** of this book about **Trader Management.**

Whatever the actual cause of an implementation error it is important to track how much profit or loss the system *should* have made compared to how much it *actually* made. Any difference is an implementation error (or deviation, **D**) and should not be taken into account when deciding whether your system is performing within expected parameters. It is no use suspending a trading system because it lost 30R when you only expected a 15R draw-down. If 20 of the 30R in losses were due to improper implementation of the system then it's the implementation, no the system, that is broken. You are fixing the symptom, not the cause, in this case and suspending a possibly perfectly good system.

⚊ Suspension

If your system does start operating outside normal parameters i.e. has a larger draw-down, or makes a much bigger profit than expected, and any difference cannot be explained by implementation errors then you may have to suspend trading the system temporarily.

In the case of making too much cash it is an indication that you are actually taking more risk than you thought you were and you should seriously consider reducing your position-sizing accordingly.

If the hypothesis that the system's idea is based on becomes invalid then you should suspend trading the system immediately regardless of performance up to that point. A full evaluation of the impact of the changes should be done to see if the system can continue to be traded in some modified form.

Continue to paper-trade the system to see how performance has been affected. Usually, at least 30 trades are required to represent any kind of reasonable sample. If the system returns to "normal" operation, then it can come out of suspension and be given a full allocation of capital again. If the system does not return to acceptable performance, or there has been such a fundamental change to the way the system should work, then it should be retired and replaced by a new system; which you should already have under development and testing right?

Another cause for possible system suspension would be that your trade setup or entry is failing to signal trades at the desired frequency. This could be due to fewer instruments being included in your instrument filter, reduced volatility for the traded market, or low volume. This is an example of a system basically suspending itself, and only time will tell if it is a temporary or permanent change for the system in question. Continue to monitor the trade signals and see if the frequency goes back to normal. If it does not recover in a pre-determined timeframe then the system should be retired.

⚡ Retirement

"When is a system broken?" is a common question for traders, and much of the answer comes from having a good simulation of what the system is "normally" capable of which was covered in detail in the section called **Using Simulation**, starting on page 108. If you know what "normal" performance looks like it is much easier to have rules in place to detect abnormal performance. Situations that should lead to a system being retired include:

- If liquidity in the system's instruments dries up permanently then a system may no longer signal any trades.

- If performance goes out of pre-determined bands and does not recover even when paper-traded for at least 30 trades.

- If the hypothesis the system is based on is permanently invalidated.

For these reasons it is usually a good idea to have some backup trading systems waiting in the wings to be given an allocation of capital if one or more of your primary trading systems has to be retired.

⚡ Trading System Performance Measurement and Comparison

The last subject I want to cover has to do with the complexity of trading multiple systems, how you determine if systems are correlated, and how to measure their relative performance.

Are systems independent or correlated?

If you are going to trade more than one system, then they need to be uncorrelated otherwise it is the equivalent of just trading one system with twice as much capital. The whole reason for trading more than one system is to provide some kind of diversification so that when one particular system is performing poorly, others may be performing well, and overall your performance will be less volatile.

Often it is desirable to trade multiple trading systems for diversification reasons. This is in the hope they will have losing periods at different times. Trading several non-correlated systems should result in a smoother equity curve. For this reason it is a good idea to know how, and why, your systems are not correlated with each other.

The main ways a system can be diversified will now be discussed.

Geography

Trading a system that operates on markets in different countries can help since regional macro-economic conditions are rarely similar and move in different directions at different paces.

Time Frame

Trading systems that operate on different time frames (tick, minute, hourly, daily, weekly, etc.) can still work because of the fractal nature of markets. A system can operate in many timeframes, each one having similarities of behavior but which are not directly correlated. The prevailing trend and volatility of a particular system can be different in each of the timeframes.

Instrument

The instrument a system is designed to trade can offer some diversification - systems that trade equities, options, futures, fixed income, or foreign exchange all have their own different 'personalities', implementation costs, margin rules, and performance characteristics.

Trade Frequency

Systems that have differing trade frequencies are generally not correlated with each other. A system that generates a signal once per day will have a different profile to one that trades once per month even if the core system is identical and trades similar instruments or markets.

Idea

The idea behind a system can be completely different to the other systems you trade. This will mean even if it is trading in the same markets and instruments, your system results may not be correlated.

Side

Systems that trade long-only, short-only, or long and short will all have different performance profiles even if there are many similarities between them. Creating systems that can simultaneously be long and short in the same markets can reduce overall market exposure and therefore reduce risk and correlation with overall market direction. Systems that can trade both long and short will generate more signals than ones that only trade on one side of the market.

Trade Duration

A system that has average trade durations of one week will perform differently than one that holds positions for a month. Your average trade duration is determined by how wide your stops are in relation to the volatility of the instrument you are trading so it is relatively easy to manipulate since your exit strategy determines this.

In all cases it is important to remember that sometimes, during panics for example, all financial instruments can move in "unexpected" directions at the same time even if they are not normally correlated. Trading multiple non-correlated systems is only a partial remedy to this problem - the other part is never trading so big so that your account will blow up if the 'perfect storm' hits all your positions at the same time and they all get stopped out as 1R (or bigger) losses.

Are Trades Independent?

Another key factor in diversification is whether your trades for each system are completely independent of each other. It is usually not a good idea to have rules that do something different based on previous trades - this introduces some built-in serial dependence in your trading systems that can reduce diversification and increase correlation. It may also reduce the validity of any simulations you perform.

The tests that were mentioned in the section on **Serial Dependency**, on page 109, should be applied across all systems to see if there is any correlation or serial dependency between all trades.

Are systems correlated with the markets they trade?

If a system is correlated with the market it trades, for example if you use a market trend indicator to enter positions, or only enter positions in the direction of the overall market, then you may be better off just trading an instrument that represents the overall market instead. For example, you could trade the S&P 500 Exchange Traded Fund (symbol SPY) instead of individual S&P 500 equities.

Performance Within Market Type

As mentioned in the section on **Trading Systems and Market Type**, on page 69, it may be true that a trading system only performs well in certain types of market. If multiple systems have similar performance profile within market type then it is an indication that their performance is correlated and not independent.

Variability of Performance

All systems go through losing periods, or periods of variable performance. If more than one system goes through a poor performing period at the same time it may be an indication of some kind of correlation.

⚐ System Correlation Summary

Generally you want to avoid trading multiple correlated systems – it's more complicated, more error prone, and you are not getting one of the main benefits of multiple systems, which is diversification. It is always a good idea to compare the performance of a system you plan to introduce to your suite of systems to all the existing ones to make sure the equity curve generated by the new system does not look identical to any of the current ones.

Trading two or more correlated systems is equivalent to trading one of them with double the size. Trading only one system with bigger size is a simpler solution to implement and manage that will result in less implementation errors.

♟ Trading System Management Summary

In **Part II** we covered in detail everything to do with the management of your trading systems. Since this is the "life blood" of your trading business it is essential that you completely understand every aspect of this part of the book and have a detailed and written plan regarding how you will create, design, test, and implement your trading systems.

The important points covered included:

- The process of trading system development and how each of the components of a trading system relate to each other.

- How important exits are in the whole of your trading system.

- How position-sizing determines how much risk you are taking and how much reward to expect.

- How simulation can be used to assess the possible variability of results and how this should affect your position-sizing decisions.

- What the lifecycle of a trading system looks like and how introduction, suspension and retirement of trading systems should be managed.

- How to allocate and manage capital across multiple trading systems and accounts.

Figure 17, on page 150, shows a summary of the lifecycle of a trading system and how it can change over time. This section dealt with each aspect of a system's life and how it can be managed.

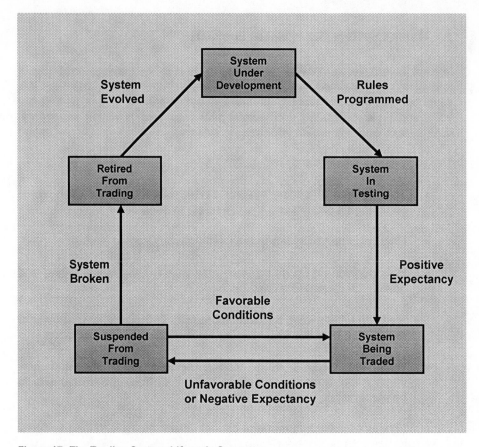

Figure 17: The Trading System Lifecycle Summary

A trading system goes from development to testing once the idea is quantified and programmed. If it has positive expectancy then it can be given a capital allocation and commence trading. If conditions are unfavorable or the system operates outside expected parameters it may be temporarily suspended. Suspended systems that do not recover may be retired. A retired system may be redesigned (or evolved) and go through the whole lifecycle again.

The developing, testing, trading, and evolving of your suite of trading systems should be a constant process in your trading business to make sure your trading adapts to changes in the prevailing market conditions and your changing requirements.

Fear and doubt

Winter 2005, Middlebury, Vermont

We are over 3 years into this now. I am competent at implementing the suite of positive-expectancy trading systems I have developed. My business is running smoothly but things are quiet. Nobody really knows PMKing Trading exists.

I'm up 12.66% in August, but go into a draw-down and end the year up only slightly. Expenses are going up – health insurance premiums have increased by over 10% every year since I started the business. Heating oil prices are up. Mortgage interest rates are up and we can't get a 30 year, fixed rate mortgage because of the age of my business, and our non-permanent residence status. Our cash reserves are now counted in months, not years, and I'm starting to doubt this will all work out.

I've been contributing to the MasterMind forum for over 3 years and people seem to like my advice but I'm still a relative nobody. I've written some articles and eBooks that I believe are pretty good and unique. But, they aren't really selling much. I studied and became a financial advisor, advertised locally for 13 weeks; not one single phone call, never mind any clients.

I want to teach people to do what I've done with my trading – I know I can help them avoid the mistakes I have made and accelerate their learning curve. Nobody contacts me. I send one of my eBooks to the major trading magazines to see if anyone is interested. No response. I have reviewed all the trading products I have found useful and joined affiliate programs and placed all the information on pmkingtrading.com. Nobody clicks through, although web traffic has increased every month since I started the site. I write a weekly blog. I'm not sure whether anybody even reads it.

I register with some career sites and look for some consulting work. Nobody wants consultants – only employees on W2s. My $164 per hour rate, from 6 years ago at the height of the technology boom, is long gone. I don't want to leave my office, suspend my business, and go and work in Manhattan for the kind of rates I can get now. It's just not worth it.

Things look bleak. I seriously doubt this will work out. I start thinking about my Plan B (which is to go back to a regular career by getting someone to offer me a job and sponsor me for another H1-B visa). I never did like Plan B that much. Maybe things will improve next year when the temperature is back above zero degrees Fahrenheit?

♔   Part III – The End Game: Trader Management

You are the thing that determines whether your systems are accurately implemented or not – if you can't implement your trading system as defined then they may as well not exist – your results will be close to random.

A trading business is a bio-mechanical machine. The biological part (the trader) is actually just as important as the mechanical part (your trading system and the technology to implement it). It is very easy to take a good, potentially profitable, trading system and make enough psychological implementation errors to lose money very quickly. This section of the book helps you understand who you are as a trader, how to match your trading systems to your personality, and how to minimize trading system implementation errors. The goal is to minimize your negative impact on your trading systems' returns by consistently, precisely, and accurately implementing each trade your systems generate.

I'm not a psychologist, nor am I formally trained in psychology, but I am human and all my trading mentor clients are as well. Therefore, I believe I have a lot of practical experience, rather than theoretical knowledge, that is relevant to trading. I understand first-hand how we, as traders, can easily mess up a perfectly good business and trading plan. This part of the book is how to avoid making yourself the perfect saboteur to your brilliant trading plans.

♜   Should you even be doing this?

Now that I've covered business management and trading system management, you should have a good idea of what's actually involved to create and operate a trading business. At this point if you're thinking "man that sounds like a lot of work" it's probably a good indication that a trading business isn't really for you. Yes, it's a lot of work to make any business successful, so it has to be something you already have a true interest and passion for. Otherwise you just won't be able to create and maintain the required level of motivation to get the job done.

⚖ Is trading the right business for you?

Do you enjoy reading trading books? How about this one? Do you read trading-related magazines? If you've ventured so far into this book then you probably answered "yes" to all those questions. But do you enjoy writing business plans, thinking about and setting up legal entities, developing trading systems, reconciling trading account statements, or doing business accounting? Trading is more than about buying and selling stuff. In fact, for a well-run trading business, the actual trade implementation is a tiny and boring aspect of the overall business. Have you got the drive and motivation to put the effort into all the mundane, business-related tasks that need to be done well to succeed?

⚖ Trading is not like a regular career

Trading is a business that is relatively simple to start. You only need cash in a brokerage account right? However, it is hard to succeed. There's no guaranteed salary or benefits, and you can end up working all year for nothing (or less than nothing if you make a loss). Is this the kind of business your finances and emotions can cope with? True, trading systems can be scalable so that you can get much more reward for the same amount of effort, but that's not much use if you've had to foreclose on your house before your systems have a chance to make big returns.

⚖ Trading your retirement account is not a trading business

You may think you are already fit to run a trading business because you've had consistent good returns in a personal brokerage account. A trading business is not the same as achieving success in personal investments (although most people can't even do that). Money at risk in an account not due to be used for many years, and all your fixed monthly expenses being covered by an alternative income source, is an "ideal" situation for trading success. You will not act or feel the same about trading full-time when your personal and business finances are on the line every day. Especially if you have to make money to pay the bills or see your cash reserves depleted on a monthly basis.

⟐ Not all personality flaws can be fixed

No matter how dedicated you are, not everyone is suited to running their own business, never mind a trading business. For example, if you are inherently lazy and can't bring yourself to work on and complete your business planning and trading system development plan then there is little chance of success regardless of how much you know about trading. If you come across a point in this book, or any other trading-related publication, that you know you need to tackle, but just can't get round to, it is a good indication that trading is not a high enough priority for you to be successful. Think about developing another type of business, or alternative income stream, that you feel more passionate about.

⟐ Time available

Creating and running a business successfully is a time consuming task. Becoming successful at anything requires time and effort and it is unreasonable to expect to become an expert trader running your own business by spending a couple of hours a week at it, unless you are talking about 2 hours per week for 10 years. Consider how much time you can actually set aside for working on your trading business. If this number seems quite low to you then it is an indication of the priority of your trading business in relation to all the other things that demand your time. How much do you really want to spend building a trading business compared to simply dreaming about "easy money"?

⟐ Cash flow

Cash flow is the main business-killer as far as I'm concerned. If your business plan assumes you will be generating excess cash (above business expenses) in less than 3 years it's too optimistic and unrealistic. This means you need 3 years cash flow in addition to your trading capital to safely start a full-time trading business if you have no other alternative source of income. This is an insurmountable problem for most people who are unusual if they have 3 months expenses set aside let alone 3 years. Please don't quit your day job and start a trading business unless you have significant cash reserves. A much more sensible approach is to work at it in your spare time with a much longer-term goal of a gradual transition from your current career and job when the trading business is generating consistent profits over, say, a ten year period.

ᴌ   Commitment

There are many obstacles to overcome to get to success. Some of them are internal (i.e. you) and some are external (i.e. family, friends, environment, financial situation etc.). Unless you have full and complete dedication to achieving your well-defined written goals for your trading business you will get distracted, disillusioned, disappointed and ultimately give up. Nobody can give you commitment - it must come from within, and simply reading a book about trading is not going to give it to you. Seriously think about your level of commitment before making any decision with your life that may be difficult to reverse.

ᴌ   Most people are just not well-suited to being traders

It is an unavoidable fact that the way most people are "wired" and the way their personal finances are setup they are basically setting themselves up to fail from the start. The rest of this book is about the main personality and psychological problems that need to be overcome or accommodated in some way in order to accurately implement your trading systems and realize any positive-expectancy you designed into them.

Do you think like a trader?

Take 1 – The Idiot

A penniless bum walks into a bar and sees a sign on the wall and jumps for joy. Before the bartender can ask him what he wants he says 'I'll see you tomorrow' and leaves.

Take 2 – The Norm

A man walks into a bar and sees a sign on the wall and smiles. The bartender asks him what he wants. The man says 'A pint of beer please'. The bartender gives him his beer, the man drinks it, pays, and leaves.

Take 3 – The Trader

A trader walks into the same bar, sees the sign, and gets a sly grin on his face. The bartender asks him what he wants. He says 'How much is beer?' The bartender says $5 a pint. The trader says 'No, not how much I have to pay, how much do you pay for beer?'

'Why should I tell you that?' says the bartender.

'I'll make it worth your while' says the trader.

'OK' says the bartender 'I pay $2.50 a pint, now what do you want?'

'I want to sell you some beer at $2 a pint' says the trader.

'How much beer?' the bartender asks.

'As much as you can take' says the trader.

'Where is it?' says the bartender.

'Oh, I don't actually have any beer, I just want to agree to sell you some'.

'You're drunk or insane' says the bartender 'Get out of my bar'.

The trader leaves in disgust muttering something about the misleading sign.

Question: **What did the sign say?**[8]

---

[8] See the end of the book for the answer

♜ Trading Mistakes

So you have a complete, effective and workable business plan. You have a complete suite of positive-expectancy trading systems and the capital to trade them. You have your fixed expenses covered by cash reserves or alternative income streams. You have the time and dedication to run your trading business. You have your contingency plan that says what you are going to do under all the circumstances you can think of. You know what normal performance is for all your trading systems and you have rules in place to tell you when they are not working. What can possibly go wrong?

You can!

All the planning is only as good as the accuracy with which you implement it. If you don't or can't take the trades exactly as your system, or systems, say you should then your results will be random and likely to lose rather than make money. It takes a lot of mental effort and dedication to consistently and accurately implement a trading plan no matter what happens and this part of the book is about how you set up formal routines to help you maintain discipline.

Trading mistakes can be classified into 3 types, all of which relate to how you implement your trades versus your plan.

Implementation Errors are anything that causes a trade to deviate from what was specified in your plan.

Deviations from your trading rules are any decisions or events that are not as you planned or you change your rules during the trading day.

Incomplete areas of your plan that you only discover when something happens, that you don't happen to have any rules for, account for the rest of the mistakes.

Trading when you, or your trading environment, are not fit to trade is also a mistake since it basically increases your chances of making one of the errors above.

♟ Identifying and Preventing Mistakes

Every trader makes many mistakes all the time. What differentiates the successful traders is that they:

a) have ways to **identify** mistakes
b) take **responsibility** for their mistakes and
c) do things to **prevent** the same mistakes happening again

⚱ Identifying Errors

Nobody can improve their accuracy if they don't know when they are making mistakes. The first step to accurate implementation is accurate tracking of errors. Every time you make a trade you should record any deviations from your system as defined for any reason. This journal will become the information source for all your error correction procedures.

Mistakes usually cost money. Only very expert or very lucky traders make money from their mistakes. If your trading system has been designed to make money and suit your requirements then deviations from it will either lose you money or not meet your objectives. Tracking errors in terms of how many R you deviate from your system as designed is an effective way to monitor trading accuracy (referred to as D for deviation). There will always be trading errors, but keeping track of the trend in the error size and rate is very useful information.

When you are a novice trader, implementation errors can more than offset any positive expectation your systems have. As you get more proficient and put things in place to prevent errors recurring, your error rate, and the severity of the errors, should decrease to some "base-line" amount. This base-line represents how good you are as a trader versus last year. All we can hope for is gradual improvement. This is not something that can be rushed or gained overnight. Some estimates are that it takes at least 1000 attempts at something to become proficient. How long should that take using your average trade frequency right now?

I trade at least 8 systems in different markets, instruments, and timeframes and I have only recently reached the 1000 trade mark.

⚱ Deviation from Rules

Technical problems, internet connection problems, and broker problems, are all normal parts of trading. All you can do is to have backups in place that "kick in" when the primary technology fails. These need to be tracked in case there is a recurring or consistent problem with one of the components of your trading environment. However, these should not normally be responsible for a significant proportion of your overall trading errors if you have a sound and complete technology contingency plan in place.

What *is* under your control are conscious deviations from your trading plan as defined. These include skipping valid trade signals, exiting positions before you should, increasing position sizes when you shouldn't, moving stops before they are hit, giving a trade "just one more day". The list could go on for quite some time. These are the errors you have to take responsibility for – it wasn't your system that failed, it wasn't your broker that lost the stop, it wasn't your computer that crashed – it was you who chose to deviate from your systems.

⚖ Incomplete Plan

If you find yourself in a situation with an open position when you think "what should I do now?" then your plan is incomplete and the situation can be classed as an error. Obviously if you have no plan then everything you do stems from the question "what should I do now?" The only answer that isn't a mistake is "write a plan".

From time to time I find that there is a missing situation in my plan and I simply analyze the situation and add it to my trading methods. This usually results in an additional entry in my checklists someplace, and an entry in my error log. Eventually my plan will become complete enough to be really useful.

⚖ Take Responsibility for Errors

The only way to improve your trading and reduce your trading errors is to take full responsibility for everything that happens in your trading environment. If your broker makes errors that cost you money (if you know of any brokers that make errors that actually make you money please let me know) then *you* chose the broker. Therefore, the cost is your responsibility.

If your trading computer blows up because you upgraded your operating system with the latest "service pack" it's not the operating system vendor's fault they sell bug-ridden flakey software. You chose to upgrade without testing the effects first.

If you take responsibility then you realize that you have the power to completely control your trading environment by your decisions. If you don't have good backup systems and contingency plans it's because you chose not to, and your operational philosophy is therefore "hope for the best".

₺ Preventing Errors

Although it is not always possible to prevent errors from occurring, it is always possible to adapt your plan to learn from your mistakes. If you believe there is actually a finite number of mistakes that can be made, eventually you will make (and thus be able to prevent) them all.

Having formal procedures that help you accurately implement your trading system is a big step towards consistency. I have a checklist of tasks that I perform on a daily, weekly, monthly, quarterly, and yearly basis that help me maintain consistency. A simplified example of my daily check list is shown on page 35.

₺ Fit for Trading

One key factor that significantly affects your error rate is whether you trade when you are 100% fit (mentally and physically). I do a mental and physical check every morning. Just assess how you feel for a couple of minutes in a relaxed environment. This is the first item on my daily checklist and I give myself a score from 1 to 7 depending on how I feel. If I'm not a 6, or 7 I try to identify the cause and see whether there's something I can do about it to get myself up to a 6 or 7.

For example, if I didn't get enough sleep last night, does a short meditation or rest make me feel better? If I have an ache or pain somewhere does a little more exercise fix the problem?

Score	Action
7	Manage existing positions Take all new trade signals Perform new system development
6	Manage existing positions Take all new trade signals
5	Manage existing positions Do not take new trade signals
4	Close losing trades Manage remaining profitable positions Do not take new signals
3	Close losing and less than 1R winning trades Do not take new signals
2	Close all open positions Do not take new signals
1	Close all open positions Do not enter new positions Suspend trading until score is 5 or higher for 1 week

Don't just accept your initial score, but attempt to change it to 5, 6, or 7. After all we want as many "fit to trade" days out of the year as possible. Prevention is much better than cure so getting enough sleep, keeping fit, not drinking alcohol the night before (or during!) trading are all good examples of preventative measures.

If something serious and semi-permanent happens to adversely affect your trading environment, or life in general, then you should suspend trading altogether until you feel better or something changes. Attempting to trade when you are sub-optimal will simply increase trading errors and lose you money in the long run. Remember that we only want to participate when we have an edge. Part of that edge is accurate implementation of our systems.

Tracking errors by your daily score is also a useful technique that may help you to decide the "cutoff" point for suspending or altering your trading. For example, if you are still making implementation errors when your score is 6, you may consider that as the point where you will not take any new signals rather than point 5 in my case.

Your own ranking and action item system will be specific to you. Mine is presented here just as a guideline to give you some ideas. Over time you will find that you generally fall into one of 3 categories:

Fully Fit	Full trading
Below Average	Don't take new signals
Poor	Close all positions and suspend trading

You could use a simplified version of the check list that just incorporates those 3 states. Whatever you do it is important you only trade when you are in good mental and physical shape to trade. Anything else is just throwing money away on the increased chance of serious trading-related errors.

♜ The Deadly Sins of Trading

Okay so nobody generally dies due to trading, so maybe deadly is a bit strong – but your cash is at stake and your business can quickly die if you let the emotions discussed in this section sabotage you.

This section is about some of the normal personality flaws and psychological problems that need to be identified and overcome in order that they don't adversely affect your trading performance. These are all normal human emotions that everyone has to some extent and need to be worked on constantly so they don't negate all your hard work on business and trading system planning.

Remember that we create our own reality by our beliefs, so if your beliefs are not useful or are actually negative to your trading then you will have little chance of succeeding. Conversely, if you try to create useful beliefs that work for you then you greatly increase your chances of success. This whole book is full of beliefs about trading that I have personally found to be useful. However, unless you read, understand, and interpret them in a useful way, they will not be relevant to you.

♟ Greed

The old clichés are the best and this one is a favorite of mine:

Bulls and bears make money; only pigs get slaughtered.

Wanting too much too quickly simply leads to taking risks that are way too big for your trading capital and cash flow situation and is a recipe for disaster. Having and maintaining reasonable expectations for what is possible from you, your trading systems and your trading business is very important.

Remember that risk and reward always go hand-in-hand so if you're planning to make 100% return on your money then you better be prepared for a total loss of capital. There is no "free lunch" of making a good return without taking any risk so don't look for it, or pretend it's a possibility.

It is normal for people to see winning streaks and extrapolate the rest of the year based on a few winners in a row. This is a big mistake. Especially if you change anything to do with your systems or methods based on a few select winning trades.

- Do not increase position size beyond what your methods say because you think you are onto a large winning streak.

- Do not mentally account for and spend all the cash you're going to make if "things carry on like this".

- Do not expect a winning streak to go on forever and make you incredibly rich.

If you are experiencing a really good winning streak then, great, pat yourself on the back for sticking to your trading plan, but don't change anything. Keep taking the trading signals, stick with your pre-defined position-sizing rules, and just try to implement your system as defined. The losing trades will come soon and you will experience a drawdown from where you are now. Each dollar you make usually has to be made more than once with trading before your "high water mark" moves up and you can be relatively sure that money is really "made". Don't let greed sabotage your trading.

Ideally you will not be dependant on trading income to pay your expenses since this is one of the major things that leads to making decisions that take too much risk. If you need to make a certain amount per month from your trading to have positive cash flow, watch your feelings of greed very closely – they will constantly be there ready to jump out when you have a couple of winners in a row.

⚴ Fear

Courage is not the absence of fear; it's still taking action despite your fears.

Fear is a very common and destructive emotion in trading. It is closely linked to regret which to me is simply fear of what has happened in the past rather than the present or future. Fear can effectively stop you from implementing your trading plan. There are many reasons why fear can creep into your trading but the main ones include:

- Trading "scared money".
- Fear of failure.
- Fear of success.

Trading **scared money** is all about your cash flow and how much you "need" from trading to pay your fixed expenses. Also a consideration is how much a total loss of your trading capital would affect your trading business and your finances in general. For my trading mentor clients I usually like to see them trading only 10% of their overall net worth, and I also like to know that a total loss of their trading risk capital would not seriously affect their overall financial situation - although it may dent their ego, and my reputation as a trading coach! If you can set up a situation where either or all of the following circumstances exist, your fear due to taking risk should be greatly reduced:

- Your fixed expenses are covered by some other income stream.
- You have a reasonable cash reserve to see your business through many months of zero or negative trading performance.
- You don't actually need to make any money from trading to be financially secure[9].

Obviously most people who want to create a trading business because their finances are far from sound to start with are under the misconception that trading for a living is "easy money". Chances of success if this is the case are virtually zero due to fear causing many implementation errors and making accurate implementation of any trading plan very difficult.

---

[9] I know this one is a bit idealistic.

Fear of **failure** is another very common cause of implementation errors and stems mainly from poor preparation which results in a lack of confidence in your trading plan. Also, having unreasonable goals or timelines for your success can undermine your confidence and cause fear. The main defenses against fear of failure are to:

- Have a complete, thorough, and achievable written plan for all aspects of your trading that you have confidence in.

- Set measures of success which are not directly to do with making money. For example: to develop a new trading system every year, to reduce your implementation errors, to reduce your fixed business expenses etc.

The last kind of fear that most people don't even consider at all is fear of **success.** How will you feel about the ways your life will change if you actually succeed at what you are trying to achieve and all your trading-related dreams come true? Will all the effects be positive or are some aspects of it (subconsciously) negative in your opinion? How will your friends and family feel about you as a successful business owner? How will you feel about yourself? It is important to have some aspects of your plan that have a positive benefit to things that are important to you to help avoid fear of success.

For example, you could plan to start a foundation that benefits local charities by donating a percentage of your net profits from trading when you hit certain profit thresholds. This can avoid the feeling that trading-related profits are just taking money out of other people's pockets, not producing anything useful or tangible, and only benefiting yourself.

In summary, fear can be a debilitating and destructive force on your trading and you must take steps to identify and deal with the inevitable fears that crop up from time to time. If you find that your error rate increases significantly after you have several winning trades in a row, it could be fear of success that is kicking in and sabotaging your results.

Arrogance

Pride comes before a fall (or your biggest drawdown ever).

While it is possible to become competent enough to be consistently successful (by your own definition of success), nobody is an expert trader that knows it all and has seen it all. No matter how complete and thorough you think your plan is, there are always areas where it is sub-standard, incomplete, or does not cover situations that may arise in the future.

In going from a novice to a competent trader we pass through the four stages of learning:

1. Conscious Incompetence
2. Unconscious Incompetence
3. Conscious Competence
4. Unconscious Competence

This doesn't mean we are better than anyone else, or than the market itself, just that we have a good plan and the discipline to implement it accurately. If you start to believe you "have this cracked" then things will go bad very quickly. Never let arrogance cause you to deviate from your plan or change your risk profile or trading systems. You always have plenty to learn about in trading since it is a lifetime's endeavor.

Doubt

Those who say a thing is impossible should not interrupt the people doing it.

There are always many people telling you something's not possible. What they really mean is that it's not possible for them because that's what they believe. What does their belief have to do with you? It doesn't matter how knowledgeable, expert, intelligent or wise those people are, what does their opinion have to do with whether you can achieve your goals for your trading business?

Doubt normally comes from an external source, telling you that you can't succeed, that you listen to due to a lack of confidence in yourself or your plan. The simplest remedy for this is to:

a) have a complete and robust plan that you are confident in
b) don't listen to anyone who has negative beliefs about what you are doing.

What is possible is only limited by your own beliefs. If you believe this is all hard work, too difficult and impossible to succeed then that will become true for you. If, on the other hand, you think that what this book has to say seems reasonable and achievable for you then that will be the case. If you doubt you can succeed then you won't. Seriously listen to your own doubts and then challenge them by having a complete plan you have confidence in. Then when doubt creeps in and attempts to paralyze you (like a milder form of fear) you can simply refer to your plan to tell you what to do.

It's all in the planning – if you don't plan and test and have confidence in your methods, then doubt will stop you accurately implementing them.

⚡ Dishonesty

Dishonesty is not about being law-abiding, paying your taxes, and not stealing to make your business profitable – it's about being dishonest with yourself about how and why your business succeeds or fails. If you blame others for your poor results you are being dishonest with yourself, passing the buck, and can never learn from and improve upon your mistakes.

If all the things that cause you to deviate from your trading plan are the fault of someone else then how can you fix those problems? Only by changing the "someone" or "something" else that is to blame. This is not generally possible because the "perfect" versions of all the external factors that affect your trading environment do not exist.

The only things you have true control over are your own beliefs, so if you accept responsibility for them, and for all the results you achieve, you can actually do something positive to change things when you don't implement your plan accurately.

⚡ Hope

Planners don't hope. Hopers don't plan.

To good traders "hope" is a four letter word. Good traders don't hope. Good traders have a detailed plan they are confident in, and attempt to implement the plan accurately. Whatever results they get they take responsibility for and accept as the reward (or not) for taking risk and being in the trading business.

Hope does not enter the equation. If you are in a losing trade you stick to your plan. If you are in a winning trade you stick to your plan. You know the market price of the instruments you trade is not under your control. Hoping a loser turns into a winner, or that a winner will get bigger, is futile. If you do have to hope something then hope you are able to stick to your plan and hope it is complete. Even those hopes are not really relevant because you should *know,* not hope, that your plan is a good one.

If you find yourself hoping something will happen to your trading it is a strong indication there's something missing in your plan and you need to do more work to find out what it is.

♟ Impatience

Whatever the answer is multiply it by Pi.

One of the annoying aspects (for me anyway) of trading for a living is the fact that it is impossible to predict (or speed up) how long it will take for "success" to appear. Unrealistic timeframes can lead to feelings of failure even when you haven't really failed.

In my experience people expect things to work out far quicker than is realistic and so they are setting themselves up for a disappointment right from the start. A good rule of thumb is to multiply time and cost estimates by Pi (that's about 3 for the non-mathematically minded readers).

For most projects or businesses if you actually did multiply your best estimates by Pi, and use that as the estimate for how long it would take and how much it would cost, the business would probably not get off the ground. Unfortunately this has nothing to do with how long it would really take, just how unrealistic people's expectations are.

If you take your initial estimates and multiply by Pi and the results you get are totally unacceptable (e.g. "There's no way I'm waiting *that* long to make money!") it's a good indication you're setting yourself up with unrealistic expectations and therefore a big disappointment.

Wanting something to be cash-flow-positive in the first year is futile if it's just not practical. Remember you have the rest of your life to make this work, isn't it a better idea to set things up so you can have 3 years to make money instead of one? Doesn't that increase your chances of success? If that's not possible for you then change things, or delay starting the business, until it does work.

There's a reason many businesses "fail" in the first 3 years – it's because their definition of success is unrealistic. Don't be impatient, let things happen in their own realistic time frame. However, keep working on the details on a daily basis and the success will happen in its own good time.

♜ The Saving Virtues of Trading

Having covered all the negative personality traits that can sabotage your trading, it's time to cover some of the ones you want to nurture and improve. Generally these are the mirror-image, or alter-ego of the bad traits but it is worthwhile going through them for extra positive reinforcement. Some people respond best to "don't do this" while others take more notice of "what good looks like". Whichever version you prefer, it is important that you identify your strengths and build on them, and work on reducing your weaknesses.

♙ Consistency

Good trading is boring not exciting.

Many trading books talk about discipline as the key to success, but I believe the really important trait is consistency. Once you have a positive-expectancy system that can be operated within a controlled trading environment, then whether you are successful or not depends entirely on how consistent you are with the implementation.

If you believe your rules and methods are the best they can be, then consistently applying them is the fastest route to success. Any deviation means you are operating in a sub-optimal way and this will slow down your journey to success.

Consistency comes from a detailed written routine for every aspect of your trading that covers every time period: Daily, Weekly, Monthly, Quarterly, and Yearly. This is as "simple" as writing down all the tasks you must perform, what time you plan to perform them, and then checking them off each and every time period. Missing a task, performing it at the wrong time, or doing it more often than it should be done are all examples of mistakes that can cost you money.

An example of my simplified daily check list is shown on page 35. The items and times that should be on yours will depend entirely on what kind of business you create and over what timeframe your trading systems operate. This may be one of the most boring tasks you have to do but it certainly can increase your chances of success, and it's actually pretty easy to create. Just operate your trading business for a month and write down everything you do. This can form the basis of your operational plan if you don't want to sit down and think about it in advance.

In any case, if you don't have written rules for what you are supposed to do, how will you know you are applying them consistently? Good trading should be boring, consistent implementation of a well-defined plan, not "seat of the pants", split-second decision making under pressure. If you're looking for excitement go sky-diving.

⚖ Integrity

You're the one who has to sleep at night with the decisions you make.

Integrity is more than just being honest, it's about "doing the right thing" for yourself and everyone else affected by your trading business. If your broker made an error in your favor on your brokerage statement would you report it just as quickly as an error against you?

Dealing with everyone and everything related to your trading with integrity is a very powerful beneficial force that can give you the strength and dedication to successfully implement your plans. If you know "deep down" you have always acted with honor and done the right thing no matter what, it can help you accept and embrace whatever results you get. Even when acting with integrity is a difficult decision, the rewards usually far outweigh the cost. I believe serendipity is simply integrity coming back to benefit you in a positive way.

Don't underestimate the importance of going beyond simple honesty in your trading business and everyone you deal with.

⚖ Confidence

If you believe you can do it then you may just be right; if you believe you can't do it then you're definitely right.

Confidence comes in direct proportion to the amount of effort and hard work you put into your trading plan, and how sound your useful beliefs about trading are. If you have made all the hard decisions, put all the effort into your trading plan, and thoroughly tested everything to the best of your ability to ensure it meets you requirements, then it is difficult not to be confident in your chances of a successful outcome.

On the other hand, if you have not spent the time and money on an adequate trading education, don't have a complete plan, haven't performed thorough testing, and don't have the discipline to consistently apply your trading methods, then it will be very difficult to be confident.

Absolute confidence in your methods is an essential ingredient to being able to trade through the inevitable losing periods your trading will go through. Trading consistently despite having a string of losers is impossible unless you have confidence and truly believe your system will recover and get back to profitability.

There is no shortcut to confidence – it is the direct result of the time and effort you have put into your business and system development coupled with the real-life positive feedback of trading your system successfully.

⚊ Patience

Success takes its own good time.

Actual trading results are something that can't be rushed. Keeping score simply by how much money you make or lose is not a good measure of success. It is much better to measure your error rate and attempt to keep it as low as possible as a measure of success and improvement.

Patience is required in trading as in every long-term endeavor. Look after each individual trade and the yearly results will take care of themselves. The "personality" of a particular trading method takes considerable time to show itself in real-time trading especially if it is a longer-term system.

Markets, and therefore systems that trade instruments within those markets, can be in prolonged trends or consolidations for significant periods of time. If these are conditions that are not favorable for your system you may get lengthy periods of zero, or negative performance which is perfectly normal.

Expecting and requiring "action" all the time is counterproductive to your trading and will cause you to deviate from your plan in order to "make something happen". If you are impatient with your trading then one possible solution is to implement a system that takes short-term trades that will fulfill your need for action, but have other non-correlated systems that take advantage of long-term market trends. This is exactly how I dealt with my own impatience with my trading.

Controlling how long it takes to hit certain profit targets or other measures of success is generally impossible, so being patient while things are working out is a very useful personality trait to have. Again this can come back to your cash flow situation and how long you have to make things work – the actual time it takes is not dependant on how long you want it to take no matter how important that is to you.

Don't set yourself up to fail by "needing" things to work out in a certain timeframe.

Humility

I'm competent at implementing my trading plan. That's it.

It's easy to get a large ego when things go well with your trading. Proving "everyone" wrong by actually not blowing up your account in 3 months is a big achievement, but it doesn't make you an expert. Having the humility to know you can't control the markets, or the results of any one trade is important to keep yourself grounded and not get over confident.

Personally I believe I am competent to implement my trading plan accurately, that it's a good plan, and that I will ultimately succeed with my trading business. That's about as much confidence as I like to have without getting a "big head". My wife is excellent at bringing me down to earth if I get over confident by reminding me how much I lost when I started trading, how long I said it would take to be consistently profitable, and how little I actually made last year trading even though the number of implementation errors I made was the lowest ever.

Humility is about understanding how you fit into the whole trading business and picture (and how significant you are in terms of the life of the universe i.e. not very). Understanding how unimportant you are is not the same as a lack of confidence. I have great confidence in my methods, I just know how much I don't know and can never control about my trading and the environment I operate in. If you ever think you have everything truly under control you are in for a big surprise.

Useful Beliefs

All we have are beliefs and that's a belief too

This whole book is full of my beliefs about trading and how to go about doing it well. Unless you think about them, take them on board, and make them your own useful beliefs then this book will be a waste of money, time, and paper to you. Everything that is contained in this book has been useful to my trading in some way, but it is important that you think about the relevance to your own specific trading and circumstances rather than taking everything as "given".

Some beliefs I have found useful:

- We create our own reality by what we believe, therefore, we can change that reality by simply changing our beliefs.

- Conventional wisdom is usually an oxymoron.

- Markets can't be controlled or manipulated, but you can choose when to enter and exit (although not at what price) on your own terms.

- Things that go up usually continue to go up.

- Things that go down usually continue to go down.

- Entry signal determines trade frequency and little else.

- Exits are what make the money.

- Position-sizing is what matches your results to your objectives.

- Risk and reward always go hand-in-hand.

- Accurate trading is boring.

- Confidence comes from a complete plan.

- Anyone can learn to make money trading.

- Trading with an incomplete plan (or no plan) is a big mistake.

- Serendipity can be created.

Creating your own list of useful beliefs about trading and life in general is a worthwhile exercise that can give you some interesting ideas for your trading systems.

♜ When Not To Trade

Although this book is primarily about how to create a successful trading business, there are times when you simply should not trade. Generally these will get picked up by your daily "self test" check list, but there are times when you just shouldn't even bother doing the check and simply suspend trading. Examples include:

- Environmental Problems
- Emotional Problems
- Internal Conflicts
- External Conflicts
- Physical Problems

♟ Environmental Problems

When something is seriously wrong with your trading environment so you cannot function "normally" you should suspend trading until the problem is resolved. For example if you are moving your offices, have some kind of natural disaster, aren't working from your normal office, your trading computer blows up, your air conditioning breaks on a stinking hot day etc.

Sometimes these are obvious things like a natural disaster, but sometimes they can be more subtle like your broker's exchange linkage slowing down to a crawl over a few months due to an overload of new clients. Being aware of and checking your environment should be on your daily checklist of things to do.

♟ Emotional Problems

Obviously if you are experiencing strong emotions due to some internal or external factor (e.g. death of a family member) you are not going to be in any fit state to accurately implement a trading system. Don't even bother. Suspend trading immediately, close all positions and fully deal with your emotions regarding the event before resuming trading.

Internal Conflicts

Sometimes there is an internal conflict going on between on of your "internal personas" that can prevent you from accurate trading. Maybe your family part is saying you are not spending enough time with them because you've been researching that new trading system during every waking hour (or reading this book for example). Internal conflicts between facets of your personality can sabotage your trading if they are not resolved. Normally these need to be specifically resolved before you can resume trading rather than hoping they will go away on their own. Techniques for doing a "parts negotiation" are beyond the scope of this book and I will refer you to an expert on trading-related psychological issues: Van K. Tharp. His products and services can be found by doing a simple internet search for his name or via the "Links" page on pmkingtrading.com. Myself and my trading mentor clients have found them to be very valuable in our climb up the trading learning-curve.

External Conflicts

Sometimes a conflict is more "in your face" than internally. For example, your boss from your "real" job may be demanding too much of your time and not leaving any for trading implementation (how selfish of them!). Managing your life so that you have enough free time to work adequately on your trading is about prioritization. Everybody has the same number of hours per day, and everybody has similar demands from external forces on their time. The successful traders will prioritize their trading so that all important factors are considered and they can reach an equilibrium in their life between their trading and non-trading activities.

Physical Problems

Trading is an emotionally and mentally demanding activity. To do it well requires you to be in good shape. If you are not 100% fit and healthy then your capacity to perform accurate trading system implementation under pressure will be severely diminished.

Don't trade if you are ill, under the influence of drugs (prescription or illegal), or alcohol. Accurate trading requires 100% concentration over short periods with long boring interludes: physically fit people are able to cope with this much better than someone who is "under the weather" or in a "mind altered state".

Don't forget that planned suspensions of trading, i.e. vacations, should be included in your trading plan to avoid "burn out". Nobody can trade 250 trading days a year indefinitely and not show signs of fatigue. Eventually you will start making mistakes due to mental tiredness simply because you haven't had a decent break from trading in a long time. In my experience you should schedule at least 2 weeks vacation every 6 months into your trading plan for optimum performance.

Don't short-change yourself, or your trading, or your plan by over-working and causing implementation errors – it's a false economy.

♖ Health Management

This brings us on to the last section in the trader management part of this book: how your health affects your trading results; specifically in the number of implementation errors you make. I have personally found that there is a direct link between trading errors and fitness, diet, and especially vices. Not drinking alcohol the night before a trading day has definitely had a beneficial effect on my trading performance. Even if you think it'll be "out of your system" by tomorrow – it's about how seriously you take your trading.

♟ Exercise

Physical fitness leads to emotional and mental stamina too. Trading is a brain-intensive activity, and the fitter your body is the less it will interfere with good thinking. Your energy level will be elevated, your stamina (physical and mental) will increase and you will be a more accurate trader.

That's not to say I'm in tip-top shape, but I know that I must keep up a reasonable level of exercise to prevent being unfit having a large negative effect on my trading. Schedule some exercise every day into your trading routine and you will see the benefits almost immediately.

♟ Diet

Linked with being fit, having a healthy diet goes hand-in-hand with getting some exercise on a daily basis. What you put in your mouth has a direct effect on your whole body including your brain. My diet would probably be too restrictive (or expensive) for most people since I am a mostly organic, lacto-vegetarian. I eat vegetable, fruits, pulses, nuts, pasta, and dairy, but no meat, fish, poultry, or other animal products.

It's hard to be out of shape eating carrots, and nothing tastes as good as produce picked fresh from your own organic garden. Seriously consider cutting out some of the highly processed, pesticide or hormone-riddled, factory-farmed, mass-produced foods that are the staple diet of many people today. Since I became a vegetarian, many years ago, I have felt physically better than I ever did before and I'm sure it has had a beneficial effect on my trading and my life in general.

♟ Vices

Everyone has vices and certain substances or products that they are addicted to. Most of these can be harmful to your trading when they are used immediately before or, much worse, during trading.

There's a reason why pilots have mandatory random drug tests and it's obvious why you don't want to be flying in a plane if the pilot has been drinking alcohol. Your trading business is no different. Do you want to be "drunk at the wheel" of your trading business and suffer the consequences, or are you serious enough about trading to abstain from certain products that may lower your performance when trading?

I personally love beer and wine, but I don't drink the night before I trade even though the effects will probably be long gone by the time I hit the "buy" button. Making a mistake because of a preventable situation is more important to me than "just one more glass of wine" on a Sunday evening.

♜ Trader Management Summary

In summary, this section discussed how you form part of your bio-mechanical machine that is your trading business. Keeping yourself in shape is every bit as important as keeping your trading computer updated with the latest security patches.

If you have created a complete and well-constructed trading plan, you are the only thing that stands between success and failure. Tracking errors and putting preventative measures in place is a key to improving over time.

Only trading when you are 100% fit for the job is also essential to long-term success. Your plan is only as good as your ability to accurately implement it. Don't short-change all your hard work by being the weak link in your trading operation.

Was it patience, confidence or stubbornness?

Fall 2006, Middlebury, Vermont

Things are working out. The company is cash-flow-positive for the year. I have trading mentor clients in the US, Canada, Australia, and South America. Every trader that has become a client is happy and wants an ongoing relationship with PMKing Trading.

I have financial advice clients. I offer them a money-back guarantee if they don't think my advice is worth the fee. Try getting that from your regular financial advisor! Everyone that comes through the door becomes a client and is still with me. It's not many, but I know I'm helping them a lot.

I become the host of the MasterMind Forum. I have an article published in the August 2006 edition of Futures Magazine. People start to know the name "PMKing Trading" in the trading business.

Finally, I can re-finance our mortgage at a fixed rate for 30 years so I can stop worrying about interest rates going up any further. Web traffic at pmkingtrading.com is still going up monthly. People are starting to click on affiliate links for the products I recommend. I have an opt-in email list of clients. My eBooks and articles are becoming more popular. Traders like my concise and to-the-point writing style and unique and useful content.

I stop looking for consulting work and Plan B stays as Plan B for the moment. I can see a light at the end of the tunnel and I'm almost sure it's not the proverbial oncoming train. I write this book. I am really hopeful that people will find it interesting and informative. We'll just have to wait and see, but right now fear and doubt have finally been replaced by confidence and expectations of success.

Let's just hope the good old United States Immigration and Nationalization Service approves PMKing Trading's E2 Visa for another 5 years. If not, we're on to Plan C – Canada here we come!

♛ Summary of Critical Success Factors

This section is a condensed summary of what this whole book is about –
and that is to succeed at creating and running your own trading business.

♛ Ability to Succeed

Giving oneself the ability to succeed by putting the time, effort, and money
into excellent trading-related education is the first step to success. This
book contains everything you need to be knowledgeable about how to
succeed. What it lacks in depth it should make up for in completeness and I
hope I have covered everything in enough detail so you know what you
have to work on.

♛ A Complete and Detailed Written Plan

As you may have noticed, every aspect of successful trading is about good
planning. A successful trading business is composed of 3 plans:

- Business Plan
- Trading Plan
- Trader Plan

Without all 3 aspects in place, success is unlikely, and results are primarily
random (i.e. due mainly to luck).

♛ Trading Edge that Overcomes Implementation Costs

As you can see from this book, your trading edge is not the foolproof entry
signal (often referred to as the "Holy Grail" in trading). Your edge is the
accurate implementation of a complete trading plan that is designed to make
money.

♛ Trading Capital and Cash Flow

Having the funds to operate the business as planned and allowing yourself
the "breathing room" to trade through the losing periods (and your learning
curve) is essential to success. Don't set yourself up to fail by requiring that
you make a certain amount of money per month by a certain, and usually
unreasonable, date.

♛ Desire to Succeed

The last thing you need is the dedication and motivation to do all the work and carry out your plans - no matter what happens.

Trading is easy when you're making money - try losing money and feeling good about it. Unless you are truly passionate and dedicated, you will never have the motivation to complete the long, but relatively simple, list of tasks that are required to create a complete and successful trading business.

I truly wish you success in your trading and hope this book has been informative, useful and beneficial to your trading journey. If this book has helped you in any way please take the time to send me feedback using the 'Contact' page on my web site at **www.pmkingtrading.com**.

Remember one of my most useful beliefs:

Those who say a thing is impossible should not interrupt the people doing it.

♔ Sample Trading System Code

The code for the sample trading systems is written in TradeStation®
EasyLanguage®. For electronic versions of these trading systems please
use the 'Contact' page on www.pmkingtrading.com.

♟ System 1: Fixed 12 Bar Exit

```
// SPX System 1 - Basic Long/Short SMA cross entry, fixed 12 bar exit

// Hypothesis:          Be long when it's going up and short when it's
                        going down
// Entry:               Close crosses SMA(12)
// Position Sizing:     Fixed 1 share
// Exits:               Fixed exit in 12 bars

variables:

int inposition(0),      // Are we in a position or not -1 short, 0 out,
1 long
int entrybar(0);        // Bar we entered on

// Check for long entry
if (inposition=0 and Close crosses above Average(Close,12)) then
begin
        inposition=1;
        entrybar=BarNumber;
        Buy ( "Buy" ) 1 share next bar at market;
end;

// Check for short entry
if (inposition=0 and Close crosses above Average(Close,12)) then
begin
        inposition=-1;
        entrybar=BarNumber;
        Sell short ( "Short" ) 1 share next bar at market;
end;


// Exit long in 12 bars
if (inposition=1 and BarNumber>=(entrybar+12)) then
begin
        inposition=0;
        entrybar=0;
        Sell ("Exit Long") 1 share next bar at market;
end;

// Exit short in 12 bars
if (inposition=-1 and BarNumber>=(entrybar+12)) then
begin
        inposition=0;
        entrybar=0;
        Buy to cover ("Cover Short") 1 share next bar at market;
end;
```

▲ System 2: High Win% Exit

Changes to System 1 shown in highlighted grey

```
// SPX System 2 - Basic Long/Short entry, exit if winner after 1 Bar

// Hypothesis:        Be long when it's going up and short when it's
                      going down
// Entry:             Close crosses SMA(12)
// Position Sizing:   Fixed 1 share
// Exits:             Fixed exit in 12 bars plus exit if winner after
                      1 bar

variables:

int inposition(0),   // Are we in a position or not -1 short, 0 out,
                     // 1 long
int entrybar(0);     // Bar we entered on

// Exit long
if (inposition=1 and ((Close > EntryPrice) or (BarNumber >
entrybar+100))) then
begin
        inposition=0;
        entrybar=0;
        Sell ("Exit Long") 1 share next bar at market;
end;

// Exit short
if (inposition=-1 and ((Close < EntryPrice) or (BarNumber >
entrybar+100))) then
begin
        inposition=0;
        entrybar=0;
        Buy to cover ("Cover Short") 1 share next bar at market;
end;

// Check for long entry
if (inposition=0 and Close crosses above Average(Close,12)) then
begin
        inposition=1;
        entrybar=BarNumber;
        Buy ( "Buy" ) 1 share next bar at market;
end;

// Check for short entry
if (inposition=0 and Close crosses below Average(Close,12)) then
begin
        inposition=-1;
        entrybar=BarNumber;
        Sell short ( "Short" ) 1 share next bar at market;
end;
```

♜ System 3: High Lose% Exit

Changes to System 2 shown in highlighted grey

```
// SPX System 3 - Basic Long/Short entry, exit if loser after 1 Bar

// Hypothesis:        Be long when it's going up and short when it's
                      going down
// Entry:            Close crosses SMA(12)
// Position Sizing:  Fixed 1 share
// Exits:            Fixed exit in 12 bars plus exit if loser after
                      1 bar

variables:

int inposition(0),     // Are we in a position or not -1 short, 0 out,
                        1 long
int entrybar(0);       // Bar we entered on

// Exit long
if (inposition=1 and ((Close < EntryPrice) or (BarNumber >=
entrybar+100))) then
begin
        inposition=0;
        entrybar=0;
        Sell ("Exit Long") 1 share next bar at market;
end;

// Exit short
if (inposition=-1 and ((Close > EntryPrice) or (BarNumber >=
entrybar+100))) then
begin
        inposition=0;
        entrybar=0;
        Buy to cover ("Cover Short") 1 share next bar at market;
end;

// Check for long entry
if (inposition=0 and Close crosses above Average(Close,12)) then
begin
        inposition=1;
        entrybar=BarNumber;
        Buy ( "Buy" ) 1 share next bar at market;
end;

// Check for short entry
if (inposition=0 and Close crosses below Average(Close,12)) then
begin
        inposition=-1;
        entrybar=BarNumber;
        Sell short ( "Short" ) 1 share next bar at market;
end;
```

♟ System 4: Inactivity Exit

Changes to System 3 shown in `highlighted grey`

```
// SPX System 4 - Basic Long/Short entry, exit if inactive loser after
6 bars

// Hypothesis:          Be long when it's going up and short when it's
                        going down
// Entry:               Close crosses SMA(12)
// Position Sizing:     Fixed 1 share
// Exits:               Fixed exit in 12 bars plus exit if inactive
                        loser after 6 bars

variables:

int inposition(0),     // Are we in a position or not -1 short, 0 out,
                       1 long
int entrybar(0),       // Bar we entered on
float profitorloss(0); // Current points profit or loss

// Calculate current points profit or loss
if (inposition=1) then profitorloss=Close-EntryPrice else
        if (inposition =-1) then profitorloss=EntryPrice-Close else
profitorloss=0;

// Exit inactive long
if (inposition=1 and (BarNumber > (entrybar+6) and (profitorloss>-10
and profitorloss<10) or (BarNumber>=entrybar+12))) then
begin
        inposition=0;
        entrybar=0;
        Sell ("Exit Long") 1 share next bar at market;
end;

// Exit inactive short
if (inposition=-1 and (BarNumber > (entrybar+6) and (profitorloss>-10
and profitorloss<10) or (BarNumber>entrybar+12))) then
begin
        inposition=0;
        entrybar=0;
        Buy to cover ("Cover Short") 1 share next bar at market;
end;

// Check for long entry

if (inposition=0 and Close crosses above Average(Close,12)) then
begin
        inposition=1;
        entrybar=BarNumber;
        Buy ( "Buy" ) 1 share next bar at market;
end;

// Check for short entry

if (inposition=0 and Close crosses above Average(Close,12)) then
```

```
begin
        inposition=-1;
        entrybar=BarNumber;
        Sell short ( "Short" ) 1 share next bar at market;
end;
```

♨ System 5: Additional Risk Management Exit

Changes to System 4 shown in highlighted grey

```
// SPX System 5 - Basic Long/Short entry, exit if inactive loser after
6 bars and ATR-based risk management stop

// Hypothesis:        Be long when it's going up and short when it's
                      going down
// Entry:             Close crosses SMA(12)
// Position Sizing:   Fixed 1 share
// Exits:             Exit if inactive loser after 6 bars and ATR-
                      based risk management stop

variables:

int inposition(0),     // Are we in a position or not -1 short, 0 out,
                       1 long
int entrybar(0),       // Bar we entered on
float stopsize(0),     // Fixed ATR stop
float stopprice(0),    // Stop price
float profitorloss(0); // Current points profit or loss

// Check for long entry
if (inposition=0 and Close crosses above Average(Close,12)) then
begin
        inposition=1;
        entrybar=BarNumber;
        stopsize=AvgTrueRange(12)*4;
        stopprice=Close-stopsize;
        Buy ( "Buy" ) 1 share next bar at market;
end;

// Check for short entry
if (inposition=0 and Close crosses below Average(Close,12)) then
begin
        inposition=-1;
        entrybar=BarNumber;
        stopsize=AvgTrueRange(12)*4;
        stopprice=Close+stopsize;
        Sell short ( "Short" ) 1 share next bar at market;
end;

// Calculate current points profit or loss
if (inposition=1) then profitorloss=Close-EntryPrice else
        if (inposition=-1) then profitorloss=EntryPrice-Close else
profitorloss=0;

// Exit inactive long
if (inposition=1 and (BarNumber > (entrybar+6) and (profitorloss>-10
and profitorloss<10) or (BarNumber >= entrybar+100))) then
begin
        inposition=0;
        entrybar=0;
        Sell ("Exit Long") 1 share next bar at market;
end;
```

189

```
// Exit inactive short
if (inposition=-1 and (BarNumber > (entrybar+6) and (profitorloss>-10
and profitorloss<10) or (BarNumber >= entrybar+100))) then
begin
        inposition=0;
        entrybar=0;
        Buy to cover ("Cover Short") 1 share next bar at market;
end;

// Check long stop
if (inposition=1 and BarNumber>entrybar+1 and Close<=stopprice) then
begin
        inposition=0;
        entrybar=0;
        Sell ("Long Stop") 1 share next bar at market;
end;

// Check short stop
if (inposition=-1 and BarNumber>entrybar+1 and Close>=stopprice) then
begin
        inposition=0;
        entrybar=0;
        Buy to cover ("Short Stop") 1 share next bar at market;
end;
```

♖ System 6: Additional Profit Protection Exit

Changes to System 5 shown in highlighted grey

```
// SPX System 6 - Basic Long/Short entry, exit if inactive loser after
and ATR-based risk management stop and trailing profit protection stop

// Hypothesis:        Be long when it's going up and short when it's
                      going down
// Entry:             Close crosses SMA(12)
// Position Sizing:   Fixed 1 share
// Exits:             Exit if inactive loser after 6 bars and ATR-
                      based risk management stop and trailing stop

variables:

int inposition(0),    // Are we in a position or not -1 short, 0 out,
                      1 long
int entrybar(0),      // Bar we entered on
float stopsize(0),    // Fixed ATR stop
float stopprice(0),   // Stop price
float profitorloss(0),// Current points profit or loss
float trailsize(0),   // Trailing stop size
float trailstop(0);   // Current trailing stop price

// Check for long entry

if (inposition=0 and Close crosses above Average(Close,12)) then
begin
        inposition=1;
        entrybar=BarNumber;
        stopsize=AvgTrueRange(12)*4;
        stopprice=Close-stopsize;
        trailsize=AvgTrueRange(12);
        Buy ( "Buy" ) 1 share next bar at market;
end;

// Check for short entry

if (inposition=0 and Close crosses below Average(Close,12)) then
begin
        inposition=-1;
        entrybar=BarNumber;
        stopsize=AvgTrueRange(12)*4;
        stopprice=Close+stopsize;
        trailsize=AvgTrueRange(12);
        Sell short ( "Short" ) 1 share next bar at market;
end;

// Calculate current points profit or loss
if (inposition=1) then profitorloss=Close-EntryPrice else
        if (inposition=-1) then profitorloss=EntryPrice-Close else
profitorloss=0;

// Exit inactive long
if (inposition=1 and (BarNumber > (entrybar+6) and (profitorloss>-10
and profitorloss<10) or (BarNumber >= entrybar+12))) then
```

```
begin
        inposition=0;
        entrybar=0;
        Sell ("Exit Long") 1 share next bar at market;
end;

// Exit inactive short
if (inposition=-1 and (BarNumber > (entrybar+6) and (profitorloss>-10
and profitorloss<10) or (BarNumber >= entrybar+12))) then
begin
        inposition=0;
        entrybar=0;
        Buy to cover ("Cover Short") 1 share next bar at market;
end;

// Check long stop
if (inposition=1 and BarNumber>entrybar+1 and Close<=stopprice) then
begin
        inposition=0;
        entrybar=0;
        Sell ("Long Stop") 1 share next bar at market;
end;

// Check short stop
if (inposition=-1 and BarNumber>entrybar+1 and Close>=stopprice) then
begin
        inposition=0;
        entrybar=0;
        Buy to cover ("Short Stop") 1 share next bar at market;
end;

// Adjust long trail
if (inposition=1) then trailstop=Highest(High,BarNumber-entrybar)-
trailsize;

// Adjust short trail
if (inposition=-1) then trailstop=Lowest(Low,BarNumber-
entrybar)+trailsize;

// Check long trail
if (inposition=1 and BarNumber>entrybar+1 and profitorloss>30 and
Close<=trailstop) then
begin
        inposition=0;
        entrybar=0;
        Sell ("Long Trail") 1 share next bar at market;
end;

// Check short trail
if (inposition=-1 and BarNumber>entrybar+1 and profitorloss>30 and
Close>=trailstop) then
begin
        inposition=0;
        entrybar=0;
        Buy to cover ("Short Trail") 1 share next bar at market;
end;
```

♟ System 7: Martingale

Changes to System 6 shown in <mark>highlighted grey</mark>

```
// SPX System 7 - Basic Long/Short entry, exit if inactive loser after
and ATR-based risk management stop and trailing profit protection stop

// Hypothesis:        Be long when it's going up and short when it's
                      going down
// Entry:             Close crosses SMA(12)
// Position Sizing:   Double number of contracts after a loser, back
                      to 1 contract if a winner
// Exits:             Exit if inactive loser after 6 bars and ATR-
                      based risk management stop and trailing stop


variables:

int inposition(0),     // Are we in a position or not -1 short, 0 out,
                       1 long
int entrybar(0),       // Bar we entered on
float stopsize(0),     // Fixed ATR stop
float stopprice(0),    // Stop price
float profitorloss(0), // Current points profit or loss
float trailsize(0),    // Trailing stop size
float trailstop(0),    // Current trailing stop price
float positionsize(1); // Number of contracts to trade

// Check for long entry

if (inposition=0 and Close crosses above Average(Close,12)) then
begin
        inposition=1;
        entrybar=BarNumber;
        stopsize=AvgTrueRange(12)*4;
        stopprice=Close-stopsize;
        trailsize=AvgTrueRange(12);
        Buy ( "Buy" ) positionsize shares next bar at market;
end;

// Check for short entry

if (inposition=0 and Close crosses below Average(Close,12)) then
begin
        inposition=-1;
        entrybar=BarNumber;
        stopsize=AvgTrueRange(12)*4;
        stopprice=Close+stopsize;
        trailsize=AvgTrueRange(12);
        Sell short ( "Short" ) positionsize shares next bar at market;
end;

// Calculate current points profit or loss
if (inposition=1) then profitorloss=Close-EntryPrice else
        if (inposition=-1) then profitorloss=EntryPrice-Close else
profitorloss=0;
```

```
// Exit inactive long
if (inposition=1 and (BarNumber > (entrybar+6) and (profitorloss>-10
and profitorloss<10) or (BarNumber >= entrybar+12))) then
begin
        inposition=0;
        entrybar=0;
        Sell ("Exit Long") positionsize shares next bar at market;
        if profitorloss > 0 then positionsize=1 else
positionsize=positionsize*2;
end;

// Exit inactive short
if (inposition=-1 and (BarNumber > (entrybar+6) and (profitorloss>-10
and profitorloss<10) or (BarNumber >= entrybar+12))) then
begin
        inposition=0;
        entrybar=0;
        Buy to cover ("Cover Short") positionsize shares next bar at
market;
        if profitorloss > 0 then positionsize=1 else
positionsize=positionsize*2;
end;

// Check long stop
if (inposition=1 and BarNumber>entrybar+1 and Close<=stopprice) then
begin
        inposition=0;
        entrybar=0;
        Sell ("Long Stop") positionsize shares next bar at market;
        if profitorloss > 0 then positionsize=1 else
positionsize=positionsize*2;
end;

// Check short stop
if (inposition=-1 and BarNumber>entrybar+1 and Close>=stopprice) then
begin
        inposition=0;
        entrybar=0;
        Buy to cover ("Short Stop") positionsize shares next bar at
market;
        if profitorloss > 0 then positionsize=1 else
positionsize=positionsize*2;
end;

// Adjust long trail
if (inposition=1) then trailstop=Highest(High,BarNumber-entrybar)-
trailsize;

// Adjust short trail
if (inposition=-1) then trailstop=Lowest(Low,BarNumber-
entrybar)+trailsize;

// Check long trail
if (inposition=1 and BarNumber>entrybar+1 and profitorloss>30 and
Close<=trailstop) then
begin
        inposition=0;
        entrybar=0;
        Sell ("Long Trail") positionsize share next bar at market;
```

```
        if profitorloss > 0 then positionsize=1 else
positionsize=positionsize*2;
end;

// Check short trail
if (inposition=-1 and BarNumber>entrybar+1 and profitorloss>30 and
Close>=trailstop) then
begin
        inposition=0;
        entrybar=0;
        Buy to cover ("Short Trail") positionsize share next bar at
market;
        if profitorloss > 0 then positionsize=1 else
positionsize=positionsize*2;
end;
```

🐚 System 8: Fixed Dollar

Changes to System 7 shown in <mark>highlighted grey</mark>

```
// SPX System 8 - Basic Long/Short entry, exit if inactive loser after
and ATR-based risk management stop and trailing profit protection stop

// Hypothesis:        Be long when it's going up and short when it's
                      going down
// Entry:             Close crosses SMA(12)
// Position Sizing:   Risk $10,000 per trade with 1 point = $50
// Exits:             Exit if inactive loser after 6 bars and ATR-
                      based risk management stop and trailing stop

variables:

int inposition(0),      // Are we in a position or not -1 short, 0 out,
                        1 long
int entrybar(0),        // Bar we entered on
float stopsize(0),      // Fixed ATR stop
float stopprice(0),     // Stop price
float profitorloss(0),  // Current points profit or loss
float trailsize(0),     // Trailing stop size
float trailstop(0),     // Current trailing stop price
float positionsize(0);  // Number of contracts to trade

// Check for long entry

if (inposition=0 and Close crosses above Average(Close,12)) then
begin
        inposition=1;
        entrybar=BarNumber;
        stopsize=AvgTrueRange(12)*4;
        stopprice=Close-stopsize;
        trailsize=AvgTrueRange(12);

// Calculate position size

        positionsize=round(10000/(stopsize*50),0);
        if positionsize<1 then positionsize=1;

        Buy ( "Buy" ) positionsize shares next bar at market;
end;

// Check for short entry

if (inposition=0 and Close crosses below Average(Close,12)) then
begin
        inposition=-1;
        entrybar=BarNumber;
        stopsize=AvgTrueRange(12)*4;
        stopprice=Close+stopsize;
        trailsize=AvgTrueRange(12);

        // Calculate position size
```

196

```
        positionsize=round(10000/(stopsize*50),0);
        if positionsize<1 then positionsize=1;

        Sell short ( "Short" ) positionsize shares next bar at market;
end;

// Calculate current points profit or loss
if (inposition=1) then profitorloss=Close-EntryPrice else
        if (inposition=-1) then profitorloss=EntryPrice-Close else
profitorloss=0;

// Exit inactive long
if (inposition=1 and (BarNumber > (entrybar+6) and (profitorloss>-10
and profitorloss<10) or (BarNumber >= entrybar+12))) then
begin
        inposition=0;
        entrybar=0;
        Sell ("Exit Long") positionsize shares next bar at market;
end;

// Exit inactive short
if (inposition=-1 and (BarNumber > (entrybar+6) and (profitorloss>-10
and profitorloss<10) or (BarNumber >= entrybar+12))) then
begin
        inposition=0;
        entrybar=0;
        Buy to cover ("Cover Short") positionsize shares next bar at
market;
end;

// Check long stop
if (inposition=1 and BarNumber>entrybar+1 and Close<=stopprice) then
begin
        inposition=0;
        entrybar=0;
        Sell ("Long Stop") positionsize shares next bar at market;
end;

// Check short stop
if (inposition=-1 and BarNumber>entrybar+1 and Close>=stopprice) then
begin
        inposition=0;
        entrybar=0;
        Buy to cover ("Short Stop") positionsize shares next bar at
market;
end;

// Adjust long trail
if (inposition=1) then trailstop=Highest(High,BarNumber-entrybar)-
trailsize;

// Adjust short trail
if (inposition=-1) then trailstop=Lowest(Low,BarNumber-
entrybar)+trailsize;

// Check long trail
if (inposition=1 and BarNumber>entrybar+1 and profitorloss>30 and
Close<=trailstop) then
begin
```

```
        inposition=0;
        entrybar=0;
        Sell ("Long Trail") positionsize share next bar at market;
end;

// Check short trail
if (inposition=-1 and BarNumber>entrybar+1 and profitorloss>30 and
Close>=trailstop) then
begin
        inposition=0;
        entrybar=0;
        Buy to cover ("Short Trail") positionsize share next bar at
market;
end;
```

♜ System 9: Fixed Percentage

Changes to System 8 shown in `highlighted grey`

```
// SPX System 9 - Basic Long/Short entry, exit if inactive loser after
and ATR-based risk management stop and trailing profit protection stop

// Hypothesis:          Be long when it's going up and short when it's
                        going down
// Entry:               Close crosses SMA(12)
// Position Sizing:     Risk 1.5% of $100,000 account value per trade
                        with 1 point = $50
// Exits:               Exit if inactive loser after 6 bars and ATR-
                        based risk management stop and trailing stop


variables:

int inposition(0),              // Are we in a position or not -1 short,
                                0 out, 1 long
int entrybar(0),                // Bar we entered on
float stopsize(0),              // Fixed ATR stop
float stopprice(0),             // Stop price
float profitorloss(0),          // Current points profit or loss
float trailsize(0),             // Trailing stop size
float trailstop(0),             // Current trailing stop price
float accountvalue(100000),     // Starting account value
float positionsize(0);          // Number of contracts to trade

// Check for long entry

if (inposition=0 and Close crosses above Average(Close,12)) then
begin
        inposition=1;
        entrybar=BarNumber;
        stopsize=AvgTrueRange(12)*4;
        stopprice=Close-stopsize;
        trailsize=AvgTrueRange(12);

// Calculate position size

        positionsize=round(accountvalue*0.15/(stopsize*50),0);
        if positionsize<1 then positionsize=1;

        Buy ( "Buy" ) positionsize shares next bar at market;
end;

// Check for short entry

if (inposition=0 and Close crosses below Average(Close,12)) then
begin
        inposition=-1;
        entrybar=BarNumber;
        stopsize=AvgTrueRange(12)*4;
        stopprice=Close+stopsize;
        trailsize=AvgTrueRange(12);
```

```
        // Calculate position size
        positionsize=round(accountvalue*0.15/(stopsize*50),0);
        if positionsize<1 then positionsize=1;

        Sell short ( "Short" ) positionsize shares next bar at market;
end;

// Calculate current points profit or loss
if (inposition=1) then profitorloss=Close-EntryPrice else
        if (inposition=-1) then profitorloss=EntryPrice-Close else
profitorloss=0;

// Exit inactive long
if (inposition=1 and (BarNumber > (entrybar+6) and (profitorloss>-10
and profitorloss<10) or (BarNumber >= entrybar+12))) then
begin
        inposition=0;
        entrybar=0;
        Sell ("Exit Long") positionsize shares next bar at market;
        accountvalue=accountvalue+((Close-
EntryPrice)*positionsize*50);
end;

// Exit inactive short
if (inposition=-1 and (BarNumber > (entrybar+6) and (profitorloss>-10
and profitorloss<10) or (BarNumber >= entrybar+12))) then
begin
        inposition=0;
        entrybar=0;
        Buy to cover ("Cover Short") positionsize shares next bar at
market;
        accountvalue=accountvalue+((EntryPrice-
Close)*positionsize*50);
end;

// Check long stop
if (inposition=1 and BarNumber>entrybar+1 and Close<=stopprice) then
begin
        inposition=0;
        entrybar=0;
        Sell ("Long Stop") positionsize shares next bar at market;
        accountvalue=accountvalue+((Close-
EntryPrice)*positionsize*50);
end;

// Check short stop
if (inposition=-1 and BarNumber>entrybar+1 and Close>=stopprice) then
begin
        inposition=0;
        entrybar=0;
        Buy to cover ("Short Stop") positionsize shares next bar at
market;
        accountvalue=accountvalue+((EntryPrice-
Close)*positionsize*50);
end;

// Adjust long trail
if (inposition=1) then trailstop=Highest(High,BarNumber-entrybar)-
trailsize;
```

```
// Adjust short trail
if (inposition=-1) then trailstop=Lowest(Low,BarNumber-
entrybar)+trailsize;

// Check long trail
if (inposition=1 and BarNumber>entrybar+1 and profitorloss>30 and
Close<=trailstop) then
begin
        inposition=0;
        entrybar=0;
        Sell ("Long Trail") positionsize share next bar at market;
        accountvalue=accountvalue+((Close-
EntryPrice)*positionsize*50);
end;

// Check short trail
if (inposition=-1 and BarNumber>entrybar+1 and profitorloss>30 and
Close>=trailstop) then
begin
        inposition=0;
        entrybar=0;
        Buy to cover ("Short Trail") positionsize share next bar at
market;
        accountvalue=accountvalue+((EntryPrice-
Close)*positionsize*50);
end;
```

♟ System 10: Averaging Down

Changes to System 9 shown in highlighted grey

```
// SPX System 10 - Basic Long/Short entry, exit if inactive loser
after and ATR-based risk management stop and trailing profit
protection stop

// Hypothesis:        Be long when it's going up and short when it's
                      going down
// Entry:             Close crosses SMA(12)
// Position Sizing:   Risk 1.5% of account value per trade with 1
                      point = $50 plus add to a loser once
// Exits:             Exit if inactive loser after 6 bars and ATR-
                      based risk management stop and trailing stop


variables:

int inposition(0),              // Are we in a position or not -1 short,
                                   0 out, 1 long
int entrybar(0),                // Bar we entered on
float stopsize(0),              // Fixed ATR stop
float stopprice(0),             // Stop price
float profitorloss(0),          // Current points profit or loss
float trailsize(0),             // Trailing stop size
float trailstop(0),             // Current trailing stop price
float accountvalue(100000),     // Starting account value
float positionsize(0),          // Number of contracts to trade
bool added(False);              // Whether we have added to a position
                                   yet


// Check for long entry

if (inposition=0 and Close crosses above Average(Close,12)) then
begin
        added=False;
        inposition=1;
        entrybar=BarNumber;
        stopsize=AvgTrueRange(12)*4;
        stopprice=Close-stopsize;
        trailsize=AvgTrueRange(12);

// Calculate position size

        positionsize=round(accountvalue*0.15/(stopsize*50),0);
        if positionsize<1 then positionsize=1;

        Buy ( "Buy" ) positionsize shares next bar at market;
end;

// Check for short entry

if (inposition=0 and Close crosses below Average(Close,12)) then
begin
        inposition=-1;
```

```
        added=False;
        entrybar=BarNumber;
        stopsize=AvgTrueRange(12)*4;
        stopprice=Close+stopsize;
        trailsize=AvgTrueRange(12);

        // Calculate position size

        positionsize=round(accountvalue*0.15/(stopsize*50),0);
        if positionsize<1 then positionsize=1;

        Sell short ( "Short" ) positionsize shares next bar at market;
end;

// Calculate current points profit or loss
if (inposition=1) then profitorloss=Close-EntryPrice else
        if (inposition=-1) then profitorloss=EntryPrice-Close else
profitorloss=0;

// Exit inactive long
if (inposition=1 and (BarNumber > (entrybar+6) and (profitorloss>-10
and profitorloss<10) or (BarNumber >= entrybar+12))) then
begin
        inposition=0;
        entrybar=0;
        Sell ("Exit Long") positionsize shares next bar at market;
        accountvalue=accountvalue+((Close-
EntryPrice)*positionsize*50);
end;

// Exit inactive short
if (inposition=-1 and (BarNumber > (entrybar+6) and (profitorloss>-10
and profitorloss<10) or (BarNumber >= entrybar+12))) then
begin
        inposition=0;
        entrybar=0;
        Buy to cover ("Cover Short") positionsize shares next bar at
market;
        accountvalue=accountvalue+((EntryPrice-
Close)*positionsize*50);
end;

// Check long stop
if (inposition=1 and BarNumber>entrybar+1 and Close<=stopprice) then
begin
        inposition=0;
        entrybar=0;
        Sell ("Long Stop") positionsize shares next bar at market;
        accountvalue=accountvalue+((Close-
EntryPrice)*positionsize*50);
end;

// Check short stop
if (inposition=-1 and BarNumber>entrybar+1 and Close>=stopprice) then
begin
        inposition=0;
        entrybar=0;
        Buy to cover ("Short Stop") positionsize shares next bar at
market;
```

```
        accountvalue=accountvalue+((EntryPrice-
Close)*positionsize*50);
end;

// Adjust long trail
if (inposition=1) then trailstop=Highest(High,BarNumber-entrybar)-
trailsize;

// Adjust short trail
if (inposition=-1) then trailstop=Lowest(Low,BarNumber-
entrybar)+trailsize;

// Check long trail
if (inposition=1 and BarNumber>entrybar+1 and profitorloss>30 and
Close<=trailstop) then
begin
        inposition=0;
        entrybar=0;
        Sell ("Long Trail") positionsize share next bar at market;
        accountvalue=accountvalue+((Close-
EntryPrice)*positionsize*50);
end;

// Check short trail
if (inposition=-1 and BarNumber>entrybar+1 and profitorloss>30 and
Close>=trailstop) then
begin
        inposition=0;
        entrybar=0;
        Buy to cover ("Short Trail") positionsize share next bar at
market;
        accountvalue=accountvalue+((EntryPrice-
Close)*positionsize*50);
end;
```

```
// Check for add to losing long
if ((inposition=1) and profitorloss<-5 and added=False) then
begin
        Buy ( "Add Long" ) positionsize shares next bar at market;
        positionsize=positionsize*2;
        added=True;
end;

// Check for add to losing short
if ((inposition=-1) and profitorloss<-5 and added=False) then
begin
        Sell Short ( "Add Short" ) positionsize shares next bar at
market;
        positionsize=positionsize*2;
        added=True;
end;
```

🔊 System 11: Scaling In

Changes to System 10 shown in `highlighted grey`

```
// SPX System 11 - Basic Long/Short entry, exit if inactive loser
after and ATR-based risk management stop and trailing profit
protection stop

// Hypothesis:          Be long when it's going up and short when it's
                        going down
// Entry:               Close crosses SMA(12)
// Position Sizing:     Risk 1.5% of account value per trade with 1
                        point = $50 plus add to winner once
// Exits:               Exit if inactive loser after 6 bars and ATR-
                        based risk management stop and trailing stop


variables:

int inposition(0),              // Are we in a position or not -1 short,
                                0 out, 1 long
int entrybar(0),                // Bar we entered on
float stopsize(0),              // Fixed ATR stop
float stopprice(0),             // Stop price
float profitorloss(0),          // Current points profit or loss
float trailsize(0),             // Trailing stop size
float trailstop(0),             // Current trailing stop price
float accountvalue(100000),     // Starting account value
float positionsize(0),          // Number of contracts to trade
bool added(False);              // Whether we have added to a position
                                yet


// Check for long entry

if (inposition=0 and Close crosses above Average(Close,12)) then
begin
        added=False;
        inposition=1;
        entrybar=BarNumber;
        stopsize=AvgTrueRange(12)*4;
        stopprice=Close-stopsize;
        trailsize=AvgTrueRange(12);

// Calculate position size

        positionsize=round(accountvalue*0.15/(stopsize*50),0);
        if positionsize<1 then positionsize=1;

        Buy ( "Buy" ) positionsize shares next bar at market;
end;

// Check for short entry

if (inposition=0 and Close crosses below Average(Close,12)) then
begin
        inposition=-1;
        added=False;
```

```
        entrybar=BarNumber;
        stopsize=AvgTrueRange(12)*4;
        stopprice=Close+stopsize;
        trailsize=AvgTrueRange(12);

        // Calculate position size

        positionsize=round(accountvalue*0.15/(stopsize*50),0);
        if positionsize<1 then positionsize=1;

        Sell short ( "Short" ) positionsize shares next bar at market;
end;

// Calculate current points profit or loss
if (inposition=1) then profitorloss=Close-EntryPrice else
        if (inposition=-1) then profitorloss=EntryPrice-Close else
profitorloss=0;

// Exit inactive long
if (inposition=1 and (BarNumber > (entrybar+6) and (profitorloss>-10
and profitorloss<10) or (BarNumber >= entrybar+12))) then
begin
        inposition=0;
        entrybar=0;
        Sell ("Exit Long") positionsize shares next bar at market;
        accountvalue=accountvalue+((Close-
EntryPrice)*positionsize*50);
end;

// Exit inactive short
if (inposition=-1 and (BarNumber > (entrybar+6) and (profitorloss>-10
and profitorloss<10) or (BarNumber >= entrybar+12))) then
begin
        inposition=0;
        entrybar=0;
        Buy to cover ("Cover Short") positionsize shares next bar at
market;
        accountvalue=accountvalue+((EntryPrice-
Close)*positionsize*50);
end;

// Check long stop
if (inposition=1 and BarNumber>entrybar+1 and Close<=stopprice) then
begin
        inposition=0;
        entrybar=0;
        Sell ("Long Stop") positionsize shares next bar at market;
        accountvalue=accountvalue+((Close-
EntryPrice)*positionsize*50);
end;

// Check short stop
if (inposition=-1 and BarNumber>entrybar+1 and Close>=stopprice) then
begin
        inposition=0;
        entrybar=0;
        Buy to cover ("Short Stop") positionsize shares next bar at
market;
```

```
        accountvalue=accountvalue+((EntryPrice-
Close)*positionsize*50);
end;

// Adjust long trail
if (inposition=1) then trailstop=Highest(High,BarNumber-entrybar)-
trailsize;

// Adjust short trail
if (inposition=-1) then trailstop=Lowest(Low,BarNumber-
entrybar)+trailsize;

// Check long trail
if (inposition=1 and BarNumber>entrybar+1 and profitorloss>30 and
Close<=trailstop) then
begin
        inposition=0;
        entrybar=0;
        Sell ("Long Trail") positionsize share next bar at market;
        accountvalue=accountvalue+((Close-
EntryPrice)*positionsize*50);
end;

// Check short trail
if (inposition=-1 and BarNumber>entrybar+1 and profitorloss>30 and
Close>=trailstop) then
begin
        inposition=0;
        entrybar=0;
        Buy to cover ("Short Trail") positionsize share next bar at
market;
        accountvalue=accountvalue+((EntryPrice-
Close)*positionsize*50);
end;
```

```
// Check for add to winning long
if ((inposition=1) and profitorloss>5 and added=False) then
begin
        Buy ( "Add Long" ) positionsize shares next bar at market;
        positionsize=positionsize*2;
        added=True;
end;

// Check for add to winning short
if ((inposition=-1) and profitorloss>5 and added=False) then
begin
        Sell Short ( "Add Short" ) positionsize shares next bar at
market;
        positionsize=positionsize*2;
        added=True;
end;
```

Recommended Reading

♛ Trading Top List

Financial Freedom Through Electronic Day Trading, by Van K Tharp

Fooled By Randomness, by Nicholas Naseem Taleb

Fortune's Formula, by William Poundstone

Market Wizards, by Jack Schwager

Mindtraps, by Roland Baruch

Reminiscences of a Stock Operator, by Edwin LeFevre

Stock Market Wizards, by Jack Schwager

Technical Analysis, by Jack Schwager

The Money Game, by Adam Smith

The New Market Wizards, by Jack Schwager

The Psychology of Trading, by Brett Steenbarger

Trade Your Way to Financial Freedom, by Van K Tharp

The Way of the Warrior Trader, by Richard D MCall

♟ Other Useful Reading

Labyrinths of Reason, by William Poundstone

Blink, by Malcolm Gladwell

The Why Café, by John Strelecky

♠ Other Useful Trading Books

Intermarket Analysis: Profiting from Global Market Relationships, by John Murphy

Investment Gurus, by Peter Tanous

Irrational Exuberance, by Robert Shiller

Japanese Candlestick Charting - Second Edition, by Steve Nison

Liar's Poker, by Michael Lewis

New Thinking in Technical Analysis: Trading Models from the Masters, by Rick Bensignor

Practical Speculation, by Victor Neiderhoffer

Rules of the Trade: Indispensable Insights for Online Profits, by David Nassar

Running Money, by Andy Kessler

Smarter Trading: Improving Performance in Changing Markets, by Perry Kaufman

The 21 Irrefutable Truths of Trading, by John Hayden

The Electronic Day Trader, by Marc Friedfertig

The Encyclopedia of Trading Strategies, by Jeffrey Katz

The Money Masters, by John Train

The Pied Pipers of Wall Street, by Benjamin Cole

The Strategic Electronic Day Trader, by Robert Deel

Trader Vic - Methods of a Wall Street Master, by Victor Sperandeo

Trading in the Zone, by Mark Douglas

What Works in Online Trading, by Mark Etzkorn

When Genius Failed: The Rise and Fall of LTCM, by Roger Lowenstein

Glossary of Terms

ADA

Average Daily Allocation. The average amount of capital allocated to a trading system calculated on a daily basis over some time period. This can be used to calculate a more representative value for the return on investment for the system.

ATR

Average True Range. The average amount of movement in price of a financial instrument over a particular time period. The ATR takes into account that the opening price of an instrument may be different than the previous closing price thus it uses a "true range" rather than simply the high minus the low for each bar.

Balance Sheet

The accounting report for a company that shows all the current assets and liabilities. A successful trading business should have a strong balance sheet where assets are greater than liabilities.

Bar

One period of price movement. Bars are generally minute, hour, day, week, month, or year.

CFD

A Contract for Difference. A financial instrument that is similar to a futures contract but is usually a derivative of an underlying equity. A buyer and seller agree to pay each other (usually daily) any difference in price of the current market price of the underlying instrument and the price at which the CFD was entered into. CFDs are not legal financial instruments in the US.

Cost of Carry

The cost of holding (or carrying) a position that is part of the implementation cost of a trade.

D

See *Deviation*.

Deviation

The difference between the expected theoretical R of a trade and the actual R. D can be used as a measure of how accurately you are implementing your trading systems.

Degree of Freedom	Each variable parameter in a trading system is a degree of freedom that specifies a particular instance of the trading system.
E	See *Expectancy*.
Expectancy	A measure of the profitability of a trading system or method. E is the average R of all the trades for a system. If E is negative the system is likely to lose money no matter how accurately you implement it. All casino games are negative expectancy.
ECN	Electronic Communications Network. An electronic order matching venue.
Equity Curve	A real or theoretical graph of account net liquidation value over time.
Exchange	A venue for matching and executing buy and sell orders.
Exchange Linkage	A connection from a broker to an exchange.
ETF	Exchange Traded Fund. A financial instrument that trades like an equity but represents a basket of instruments like an index or sector or industry.
Instrument	A financial product that can be bought or sold for a particular price. Equities, options, fixed income (bonds), futures, and foreign exchange (FX) are the main types of financial instrument.
LLC	Limited Liability Company. A legal entity structure that has limited liability for the owners.
Moving Average	The average of a series of values over time. The average is usually recalculated periodically using the last N values thus it "moves" through time.
Optimization	The process of setting the best parameter values for each degree of freedom in a trading system to meet specified objectives.
Portfolio Heat	A measure of the worse-case loss a portfolio should sustain under normal circumstances.
R	Profit or loss for a closed trade per unit risk measured by the initial amount that could be lost if your initial exit point was hit.
Serial Dependency	A measure of how dependent the outcome of a particular trade is relative to previous trades.

Simulation	A technique that randomizes the ordering of real or theoretical trades in some way to attempt to demonstrate the variability of possible results from trading the system.
Slippage	The difference in the price signaled by a trading system and the actual price achieved when buying or selling a financial instrument. This value is usually a negative effect on your trading system and is therefore included as an implementation cost.
SMA	Simple Moving Average. A moving average calculated by using a simple mean of the values rather than a more sophisticated or complicated calculation. Normally this indicator refers to a moving average of price.
Spread	The difference between the current buying price and selling price of a financial instrument. The spread is an implementation cost since each trade will have at least one buy and sell, and the cost of implementation is the spread times the size of the trade.
System Value	A relative measure of the profitability of a trading system or method
V	See *System Value*.
VIX	Volatility Index. An index that represents current volatility that uses the current implied volatility of S&P 500 index options.
Volatility	A measure of the variability in price over some time period of a financial instrument. Average True Range (ATR) is a common measure of volatility.

Index

215

Notes

Notes

Notes

Notes

Notes

Notes

Notes

Notes

Notes

Notes

Notes

Notes

Notes

Notes

Answer to '*Do You Think Like a Trader?*' riddle on page 156:

"Free Beer Tomorrow"

Wishing you success with your trading.

Paul King
PMKing Trading LLC
www.pmkingtrading.com

LaVergne, TN USA
08 October 2010

200046LV00005B/145/A